SPORTS CHAPLAINCY

The Transformative Role of Sports Chaplaincy

Dr. Maxwell Shimba

Printed by Shimba Publishing LLC
Printed in the United States of America

TABLE OF CONTENTS

INTRODUCTION

Definition of Sports Chaplaincy

Sports chaplaincy is a specialized ministry that serves the spiritual, emotional, and moral needs of athletes, coaches, and the wider sports community. It integrates faith into the high-pressure world of sports, offering guidance, encouragement, and a sense of purpose beyond the game. A sports chaplain is often seen as a spiritual coach, a counselor, and a trusted confidant who brings faith-based support into the competitive and demanding environment of sports.

Chaplains provide pre-game prayers, lead Bible studies, offer personal counseling, and are present during life's critical moments, whether it be victory, defeat, injury, or personal crisis. Their mission extends beyond the scoreboard, aiming to nurture holistic well-being and faith within the sports arena.

History of Sports Chaplaincy

The roots of sports chaplaincy can be traced back to the early 20th century, when faith and sports began to intersect more intentionally. Christian organizations like the YMCA played a foundational role in integrating Christian values into sports, promoting the idea of building character and fostering community through athletic activities.

The formal role of a sports chaplain, however, gained prominence in the mid-20th century, particularly in the United States and the United Kingdom. Organizations like the Fellowship of Christian Athletes (FCA), founded in 1954, and Sports Chaplaincy UK, established in the 1990s, provided a platform for integrating spirituality into professional and amateur sports.

One of the landmark moments in sports chaplaincy history came when Billy Graham, a renowned evangelist, addressed athletes during major sporting events, highlighting the importance of faith in their lives. This inspired the growth of chaplaincy roles across sports leagues, from local clubs to professional teams.

Today, sports chaplaincy is a global phenomenon. Major sports organizations, including the National Football League (NFL), National Basketball Association (NBA), and international soccer clubs, employ chaplains to support players and staff. This ministry has expanded beyond traditional Christian roots to accommodate diverse faiths, ensuring spiritual care for all members of the sports community.

The Need for Sports Chaplaincy

The high-stress, competitive nature of sports can take a toll on the mental, emotional, and spiritual well-being of athletes. From the pressure to perform to the challenges of injury and retirement, athletes often face unique struggles that require specialized support. Sports chaplains play a vital role in addressing these challenges, offering a listening ear, spiritual guidance, and a message of hope and resilience.

By serving as a bridge between faith and sports, chaplains help athletes and coaches find purpose and identity beyond the accolades and achievements, fostering a sense of unity, compassion, and integrity within the sports community.

This introduction sets the stage for exploring the inspiring and impactful stories of sports chaplaincy, highlighting the transformative power of faith on and off the field.

Sports chaplaincy is a ministry dedicated to serving the spiritual, emotional, and moral needs of athletes, coaches, teams, and sports organizations. It is a unique role that integrates faith into the athletic world, offering a steady presence in the often high-pressure, competitive environment of sports.

A sports chaplain is more than just a religious figure—they are spiritual mentors, counselors, and confidants who walk alongside individuals in their personal and professional lives. They lead prayers, conduct Bible studies, provide pastoral care, and offer guidance during moments of triumph, defeat, injury, or personal crisis. The ultimate goal is to nurture the spiritual well-being of those involved in sports while fostering character development, resilience, and purpose beyond competition.

While the roots of sports chaplaincy lie in Christian traditions, the role has evolved to embrace diverse faiths, providing care for athletes and staff from various religious and cultural backgrounds.

History of Sports Chaplaincy

The concept of sports chaplaincy has its origins in the early 20th century, when the relationship between faith and athletics began to gain prominence. Christian organizations like the YMCA and the Muscular Christianity movement championed the idea that sports could build both physical strength and moral character. These early initiatives laid the groundwork for the integration of faith into athletic life.

The Rise of Formal Sports Chaplaincy

The formal establishment of sports chaplaincy as a dedicated ministry came later, particularly in the mid-20th century. The Fellowship of Christian Athletes (FCA), founded in 1954 in the United States, was a pioneering organization in this field. It sought to unite faith and sports, providing resources and mentorship for athletes. Similarly, Athletes in Action, established in 1966, focused on evangelism and discipleship through sports.

In the United Kingdom, the development of sports chaplaincy took a significant step with the establishment of Sports Chaplaincy UK in the 1990s. This organization created a structured network of chaplains serving professional and amateur sports clubs across the country, providing a model for sports chaplaincy worldwide.

Influential Figures and Milestones

Renowned evangelist Billy Graham was instrumental in popularizing the idea of sports chaplaincy. His ministry often addressed athletes during major events, emphasizing the role of faith in their personal and professional lives. This inspired sports organizations to formally include chaplaincy services.

The inclusion of chaplains in professional sports leagues, such as the National Football League (NFL) and Major League Baseball (MLB), further solidified the role. Over time, chaplaincy expanded to other sports, including basketball, soccer, cricket, and rugby, becoming an integral part of team culture.

Modern-Day Chaplaincy

Today, sports chaplaincy is a global phenomenon, with chaplains serving at all levels of sports, from youth leagues to the Olympics. The role has expanded to include support for issues such as mental health, diversity, and life transitions, ensuring holistic care for the sports community.

Through decades of growth and adaptation, sports chaplaincy has proven to be a vital ministry, bringing faith and encouragement to the world of sports and making a lasting impact on countless lives.

THE ROLE OF A SPORTS CHAPLAIN IN THE ATHLETIC COMMUNITY

A sports chaplain plays a multifaceted and indispensable role in the athletic community, serving as a bridge between faith and sports while offering support that extends beyond the confines of the playing field. Their presence provides athletes, coaches, and staff with spiritual guidance, emotional care, and moral support, helping them navigate the unique challenges of the sports world.

A Spiritual Guide

At its core, the role of a sports chaplain is to serve as a spiritual mentor and guide. They provide athletes and coaches with opportunities to explore and deepen their faith, offering resources such as prayer, Bible studies, and worship services. Through these activities, chaplains help foster a sense of purpose and perspective, encouraging individuals to see beyond their athletic achievements to their broader identity and calling.

Chaplains also emphasize values like humility, integrity, and gratitude, helping athletes integrate their faith into their daily lives and decisions. By nurturing spiritual growth, they create an environment where faith becomes a source of strength, resilience, and inspiration.

Emotional and Pastoral Support

The high-pressure nature of sports can bring significant emotional and mental challenges, from the stress of competition to the impact of injuries, losses, or public scrutiny. A sports chaplain offers a listening ear and a compassionate presence, providing emotional and pastoral care during these critical moments.

Whether comforting a player recovering from a career-threatening injury or helping a team process the loss of a teammate, chaplains are often the first point of contact for emotional and spiritual needs. They provide encouragement during slumps, celebrate triumphs, and offer hope and perspective in times of personal or professional crisis.

Moral and Ethical Leadership

Sports chaplains also serve as moral and ethical leaders within the athletic community. By teaching and modeling principles such as fairness, respect, and teamwork, they help create a culture of integrity. Athletes and coaches often turn to chaplains for guidance on ethical dilemmas, whether related to competition, relationships, or off-field behavior.

In this way, chaplains help ensure that the values of the team or organization align with broader principles of character and good conduct, fostering an environment where individuals are encouraged to make decisions based on integrity rather than convenience.

Building Relationships and Trust

The role of a sports chaplain is deeply relational. They invest time in building trust with athletes, coaches, and staff, creating a safe and supportive space where individuals feel comfortable sharing their struggles and aspirations. By consistently showing care and concern, chaplains become a trusted part of the team, often forming bonds that last long after an athlete's playing career ends.

Chaplains are often present at pivotal moments—before games, during training sessions, and in the locker room— allowing them to become an integral part of the athletic journey. These relationships are the foundation of their ministry, enabling them to provide impactful and personalized support.

Advocates for Holistic Well-Being

In addition to spiritual and emotional care, sports chaplains advocate for the holistic well-being of the athletic community. They encourage balance between the physical, mental, and spiritual aspects of life, reminding athletes that their worth is not solely defined by their performance on the field.

By addressing all dimensions of a person's life, chaplains help athletes and coaches find a sense of fulfillment and peace, whether they are in the middle of their career or transitioning to life beyond sports.

Conclusion

A sports chaplain's role is both profound and transformative, offering guidance that shapes individuals and teams not only as athletes but as people of faith and character. Their contributions enrich the athletic community, providing hope, encouragement, and purpose that extends far beyond the game.

THE IMPORTANCE OF SPIRITUALITY IN SPORTS

Sports have long been celebrated as a physical pursuit, emphasizing competition, endurance, and skill. Yet, beneath the surface of every game, there exists a deeper layer that connects athletes to their values, emotions, and purpose: spirituality. The integration of spirituality into sports not only enhances individual performance but also fosters character development, unity, and a sense of meaning beyond the scoreboard.

Building Inner Strength

Spirituality provides athletes with an inner reservoir of strength, helping them navigate the physical and mental demands of competition. It offers a foundation for resilience, enabling them to persevere in the face of challenges, setbacks, or injuries.

For many athletes, faith becomes a source of motivation and confidence, reminding them of their greater purpose and helping them maintain focus amidst the pressures of high-stakes performance. The calming effect of spiritual practices—prayer, meditation, or reflection—helps athletes center themselves, manage stress, and maintain composure under pressure.

Fostering Humility and Gratitude

In the competitive world of sports, where accolades and achievements often take center stage, spirituality fosters humility and gratitude. Athletes who view their talents as gifts often express appreciation for the opportunity to compete and inspire others.

Spirituality shifts the focus from individual glory to collective impact, encouraging athletes to use their platform to uplift others, promote goodwill, and exemplify values like kindness, respect, and fairness. It also helps them maintain perspective, recognizing that their identity and worth are not solely tied to their performance.

Enhancing Team Unity

Sports are not just individual pursuits; they are profoundly communal experiences. Spirituality plays a pivotal role in fostering team unity and camaraderie. Shared values and collective faith practices—such as pre-game prayers or moments of reflection—create bonds that strengthen trust and collaboration among teammates.

By emphasizing principles like forgiveness, empathy, and selflessness, spirituality encourages athletes to prioritize the success of the team over personal ambition, contributing to a supportive and cohesive team environment.

Guiding Moral and Ethical Behavior

The ethical dilemmas that arise in sports—such as fair play, respect for opponents, and the use of performance-enhancing substances—are often navigated through the lens of spirituality. Spirituality provides a moral compass, guiding athletes to make decisions rooted in integrity and accountability.

Chaplains and spiritual mentors help athletes reflect on the ethical dimensions of their actions, fostering a culture of sportsmanship and respect both on and off the field. This moral framework not only benefits individuals but also elevates the reputation of sports as a whole.

Providing Perspective in Triumph and Defeat

The highs and lows of sports can be emotionally overwhelming. Victories may bring fleeting joy, while defeats can lead to frustration or self-doubt. Spirituality offers a steady perspective, reminding athletes of the bigger picture.

In moments of triumph, it instills gratitude and humility, encouraging athletes to celebrate responsibly and honorably. In times of defeat, it provides solace and hope, helping them view setbacks as opportunities for growth rather than as the end of their journey.

Bridging Life and Legacy

Sports are a temporary phase in an athlete's life, but spirituality offers a bridge to lasting legacy. By rooting their identity in their faith and values, athletes can transition from their careers with a sense of purpose and fulfillment. Spirituality encourages athletes to think beyond their achievements, focusing on the positive impact they can make on their communities and the world.

Conclusion

The importance of spirituality in sports cannot be overstated. It enriches the athletic experience, equipping individuals with the strength, perspective, and character needed to excel on and off the field. Whether through personal faith, shared practices, or moral guidance, spirituality elevates sports to a realm where values and virtues shine just as brightly as victories and records.

DR. MAXWELL SHIMBA

CHAPTER 01

THE CALLING

Discovering the Calling

The journey to becoming a sports chaplain begins with an internal awakening—a sense of purpose that aligns faith with a passion for serving others within the world of sports. Unlike conventional careers, the role of a sports chaplain often emerges as a calling, a spiritual nudge that compels individuals to step into a ministry dedicated to athletes, coaches, and teams. Discovering this calling requires introspection, prayer, and a willingness to follow where God leads.

Listening to the Inner Voice

The calling to sports chaplaincy often starts as an inner prompting, a persistent sense that God is directing your path toward a unique ministry. For some, this might arise from a deep love for sports combined with a strong desire to serve others. For others, it may come through personal experiences, such as witnessing the struggles athletes face or feeling the need for spiritual guidance in competitive environments.

This inner voice is often reinforced through prayer and reflection. By seeking God's guidance, potential chaplains begin to discern whether this sense of purpose aligns with His plan for their lives. Scripture can also illuminate the path, offering wisdom and reassurance that the desire to serve in this capacity is part of a divine mission.

"For we are God's handiwork, created in Christ Jesus to do good works, which God prepared in advance for us to do." (Ephesians 2:10)

Recognizing Your Gifts

Discovering the calling involves an honest evaluation of your God-given talents and spiritual gifts. A sports chaplain needs a unique combination of qualities: empathy, strong communication skills, a deep understanding of faith, and a passion for building relationships.

Ask yourself:

- Do I have a heart for ministry and a love for sports?
- Am I naturally drawn to mentoring and guiding others?
- Do I feel fulfilled when I help others navigate their spiritual and emotional challenges?

If the answers to these questions resonate, it may be a sign that sports chaplaincy is your calling. Recognizing your gifts is a pivotal step in understanding how you can uniquely contribute to the lives of athletes and teams.

Finding Confirmation in Community

The calling to sports chaplaincy is often confirmed through interactions with others. Mentors, pastors, and trusted friends can provide valuable insights, affirming your passion and encouraging your pursuit of this ministry.

Many who feel the call to chaplaincy find clarity through involvement in their local church, sports leagues, or faith-based organizations. Volunteering to serve in these settings allows you to test the waters and determine whether the role of a spiritual guide in the sports community aligns with your skills and passions.

Responding to Opportunities

Sometimes, the calling becomes clear when unexpected opportunities arise. You may find yourself in situations where athletes or coaches seek your advice, ask for prayer, or open up about personal struggles. These moments can serve as a divine confirmation that you are meant to step into the role of a chaplain.

Additionally, opportunities to engage in formal training or certification programs in sports chaplaincy can provide the tools and confidence needed to fully embrace the calling. Organizations like the Fellowship of Christian Athletes (FCA) or Sports Chaplaincy UK offer resources that help individuals prepare for this unique ministry.

Overcoming Doubts and Fears

Discovering the calling often involves overcoming doubts and fears. You might question your qualifications or worry about stepping into the unknown. It's important to remember that the calling is not about perfection but about obedience and faith. God equips those He calls, providing the strength, wisdom, and opportunities to fulfill His purpose.

"Trust in the Lord with all your heart and lean not on your own understanding; in all your ways submit to Him, and He will make your paths straight." (Proverbs 3:5-6)

Embracing the Mission

Once the calling is recognized and affirmed, the next step is to embrace it wholeheartedly. This means committing to a journey of growth, service, and faith. Becoming a sports chaplain is not merely a career choice but a lifelong mission to bring God's presence into the world of sports, offering hope, guidance, and love to those who need it most.

Conclusion

Discovering the calling of a sports chaplain is a deeply personal and spiritual journey. It requires prayerful discernment, self-awareness, and a willingness to follow God's direction. By listening to His voice, recognizing your gifts, and responding to opportunities, you can step into a role that has the power to transform lives and bring faith to the forefront of the athletic community.

PERSONAL STORIES OF CHAPLAINS DISCOVERING THEIR CALLING

The journey to becoming a sports chaplain is unique for every individual, often marked by personal experiences, divine nudges, and moments of clarity. The following true and verifiable stories provide a glimpse into how various chaplains discovered their calling, serving as testimonies to the power of faith and purpose in this vital ministry.

John Long: A Coach Turned Chaplain

John Long, a former college basketball coach, never imagined his career would lead him to chaplaincy. During his time as a coach, John often found himself counseling players on issues unrelated to basketball—family problems, academic stress, and personal doubts. He noticed that these moments of connection often carried a spiritual undertone.

John shared, *"I realized that what the players needed most wasn't just strategy or motivation on the court. They needed someone to point them toward hope, to remind them that their value wasn't just in their performance."*

After years of coaching, John felt a strong pull toward ministry. He enrolled in seminary and later partnered with the Fellowship of Christian Athletes (FCA). Today, John serves as a sports chaplain for several high school teams, using his experience as a coach to connect with athletes on a personal and spiritual level.

Roxanne Stone: From Athlete to Advocate

Roxanne Stone was a competitive soccer player whose life changed dramatically after a career-ending injury. Devastated by the loss of her athletic identity, she turned to her faith for comfort. During her recovery, Roxanne began volunteering with a youth soccer league, offering encouragement and mentorship to young players.

One day, a struggling player confided in her about family issues, and Roxanne prayed with her for the first time. *"That moment opened my eyes,"* Roxanne said. *"I realized that God was calling me to be more than just a mentor. I was meant to guide these kids spiritually."*

Roxanne later completed chaplaincy training and now serves as a sports chaplain for local leagues. Her story resonates with athletes who face setbacks, proving that God can use even the most painful experiences to reveal a greater purpose.

Steve Johnson: A Chaplain for the NFL

Steve Johnson's journey to chaplaincy began with a simple invitation. As a young pastor, Steve was asked to deliver a pre-game devotional for a professional football team. Initially hesitant, he accepted the opportunity, sharing a message on perseverance and faith.

After the devotional, several players approached him with personal questions about faith and life challenges. Steve recalls, *"I saw how hungry these athletes were for something deeper than the game. They wanted answers about life, purpose, and God."*

Encouraged by this experience, Steve pursued a full-time role as a sports chaplain. Today, he works with NFL teams, providing spiritual guidance, conducting Bible studies, and supporting players through life's highs and lows. His ministry has had a profound impact, helping athletes find balance and purpose beyond the field.

Angela Carter: Finding God's Call in Tragedy

Angela Carter's path to chaplaincy was shaped by tragedy. As a college track athlete, Angela lost a teammate to a sudden accident. Struggling to make sense of the loss, she turned to her faith community for solace. During this time, Angela felt compelled to help her teammates process their grief and find hope.

Angela reflected, *"God showed me that my teammates needed more than words of comfort—they needed spiritual reassurance."*

After graduating, Angela pursued chaplaincy training and began working with college athletic programs. Her ability to empathize with athletes during times of crisis has made her a trusted spiritual advisor, proving that God can turn pain into purpose.

David Sellers: Inspired by a Role Model

David Sellers grew up admiring his high school's sports chaplain, a man named Tim. Tim's unwavering support for athletes—praying with them before games, counseling them during tough times, and celebrating their victories—left a lasting impression on David.

Years later, as David pursued a career in ministry, he felt called to follow in Tim's footsteps. He said, *"Tim showed me what it meant to be a servant leader. I wanted to give athletes the same kind of encouragement and guidance that he gave me."*

David now serves as a sports chaplain for a high school and college in his hometown, often drawing inspiration from the mentorship he received as a young athlete.

Conclusion

These personal stories highlight the diverse ways God calls individuals to sports chaplaincy. Whether through personal struggles, career changes, or the influence of mentors, chaplains discover their calling by listening to God's voice and embracing opportunities to serve. Their journeys demonstrate that chaplaincy is not just a profession but a ministry born out of faith, compassion, and a deep desire to impact lives in the world of sports.

THE IMPORTANCE OF SPIRITUALITY IN SPORTS

Enhancing Sporting Performance, Personal Growth, and Well-Being

Spirituality has emerged as a critical factor in understanding the psychological and emotional dimensions of sports. As athletes navigate the pressures of competition, the pursuit of personal excellence, and the challenges of physical and mental fatigue, spirituality offers a profound means of enhancing performance, fostering personal growth, and supporting overall well-being.

The Nexus of Spirituality, Religion, and Psychology in Sports

Research consistently demonstrates that spirituality—whether expressed through organized religion or personal belief systems—has a significant impact on athletic performance and psychological resilience. By addressing fundamental human needs for purpose, connection, and inner peace, spirituality contributes to an athlete's holistic development.

A study published in the *Journal of Sport and Exercise Psychology* (2019) found that athletes who integrated spiritual practices such as prayer, meditation, or mindfulness into their routines reported higher levels of mental clarity, stress management, and emotional control. Similarly, spirituality has been linked to increased motivation and focus, as athletes view their endeavors as part of a larger, meaningful journey rather than isolated events.

Enhancing Sporting Performance

Spirituality's impact on performance stems from its ability to strengthen mental fortitude and emotional regulation. Key ways in which spirituality enhances athletic performance include:

1. Boosting Mental Resilience

Spirituality equips athletes with tools to handle stress and adversity. Practices like prayer and meditation enhance focus, reduce anxiety, and promote positive self-talk, all of which are essential for peak performance under pressure.

For instance, mindfulness-based interventions have been shown to improve performance in high-stress sports environments by cultivating a state of flow—a psychological state where athletes perform at their best without conscious effort. This state, often described as being "in the zone," aligns with spiritual practices that encourage present-moment awareness and trust in a higher power or greater purpose.

2. Promoting Goal Setting and Perseverance

Spiritual beliefs often emphasize values like discipline, perseverance, and the pursuit of excellence, which align with the principles of athletic training. Athletes who view their talents as gifts to be nurtured for a higher purpose are more likely to set ambitious goals and remain committed to achieving them.

3. Enhancing Team Cohesion

In team sports, shared spiritual practices can foster unity and trust. Pre-game prayers, communal rituals, or shared moments of reflection create bonds that strengthen team dynamics. Research suggests that athletes who feel a sense of belonging and connection to their team are more likely to perform cohesively and collaboratively.

Fostering Personal Growth

Spirituality plays a transformative role in personal development by encouraging self-reflection, ethical decision-making, and a deeper understanding of identity.

1. Building Character and Integrity

Many athletes credit their spiritual beliefs with shaping their character, guiding them toward honesty, humility, and compassion. By viewing competition as an opportunity to glorify a higher power or serve as a role model, athletes develop a sense of responsibility that extends beyond the game.

2. Encouraging Self-Awareness

Spiritual practices often involve introspection, helping athletes understand their strengths, weaknesses, and motivations. This self-awareness not only enhances performance but also promotes personal growth by encouraging athletes to align their actions with their values.

3. Overcoming Adversity

Spirituality provides a source of hope and resilience during challenging times, such as injuries, losses, or transitions out of sports. Athletes often draw strength from their faith to view setbacks as opportunities for growth, allowing them to emerge stronger and more focused.

Supporting Overall Well-Being

In addition to its impact on performance and growth, spirituality contributes to an athlete's overall well-being by addressing their emotional, mental, and social needs.

1. Reducing Stress and Anxiety

Spiritual practices like prayer, mindfulness, and gratitude have been shown to lower cortisol levels and improve emotional regulation. Athletes who incorporate these practices into their routines experience greater mental clarity and a sense of calm, even in high-pressure situations.

2. Promoting Holistic Health

Spirituality encourages a balanced approach to life, emphasizing the importance of mental, emotional, and physical health. Athletes who prioritize their spiritual well-being are more likely to adopt healthy habits, such as maintaining proper nutrition, getting adequate rest, and managing stress effectively.

3. Strengthening Social Connections

Spirituality often fosters a sense of community and belonging, whether through shared rituals, team prayers, or interactions with chaplains and mentors. These connections provide emotional support and encouragement, contributing to an athlete's overall happiness and fulfillment.

Empirical Evidence Supporting Spirituality in Sports

Numerous studies have explored the intersection of spirituality, religion, and athletic performance. Key findings include:

- **Enhanced Mental Health**: A meta-analysis published in the *Psychology of Sport and Exercise* (2020) revealed that athletes who practiced spirituality or religion reported lower levels of depression and anxiety compared to those who did not.
- **Improved Recovery**: Research in the *Journal of Athletic Training* (2018) found that athletes who engaged in spiritual practices during injury recovery experienced faster emotional healing and maintained a positive outlook.
- **Increased Motivation**: A study in the *International Journal of Sport Psychology* (2017) highlighted that athletes with strong spiritual beliefs were more motivated to train consistently and achieve long-term goals.

Conclusion

Spirituality is a cornerstone of athletic excellence, offering tools for performance enhancement, personal growth, and well-being. By addressing the mental, emotional, and social dimensions of sports, spirituality equips athletes to navigate the complexities of competition with resilience and purpose. As research continues to illuminate its benefits, the role of spirituality in sports will remain a vital area of focus for athletes, coaches, and chaplains alike.

CHAPTER 02

Integrating Faith and Sports

The integration of faith into sports has long been a transformative approach for athletes, coaches, and teams worldwide. Faith provides a foundation for personal growth, resilience, and community bonding, transcending the boundaries of the game. For chaplains like Semi, the journey of integrating faith and sports goes beyond religious rituals— it involves fostering a culture of spirituality that enriches both individual and team dynamics.

Faith as a Cornerstone of Support

As a sports chaplain, Semi describes his role as multifaceted, offering spiritual and emotional support not only to players but also to coaches, managers, and other team staff. This inclusivity emphasizes the chaplain's function as a unifying presence, bridging the gap between diverse individuals with varying levels of faith.

Semi's role often includes:

- **Devotions and Prayers**: Opening team meetings with devotions and prayers to set a tone of purpose and humility.
- **Pastoral Care**: Providing counseling and support for personal challenges, both on and off the field.
- **Faith-Based Encouragement**: Offering spiritual guidance that helps individuals see the bigger picture of their lives and careers.

This approach reflects the importance of faith in creating a holistic environment where team members feel valued beyond their athletic abilities.

Cultural Context: Faith in Fijian Rugby

For many Fijian athletes, faith is deeply ingrained in their culture. Semi highlights that in Fiji, acknowledging God at the start of a rugby match is not only common but expected. This practice creates a sacred space where athletes publicly recognize their dependence on a higher power for strength, guidance, and success.

Semi's experience with The Island Brothers rugby team illustrates this beautifully. Initially, some players were unfamiliar with devotions as part of their team meetings. However, the consistent practice of opening meetings with a devotional message quickly resonated with them.

Semi shares, *"Now when we begin our meetings, they are like, 'Hey, we need the devotion first!' The team members are now the ones driving how we start our time together."*

This shift reflects the power of faith to not only inspire individuals but also to create collective momentum. When athletes experience the benefits of integrating faith into their routines, they often become the catalysts for continuing these practices.

Faith and Performance: A Symbiotic Relationship

Faith serves as a stabilizing force in the high-pressure world of sports. By integrating spiritual practices into their routines, athletes and teams often find renewed focus, emotional balance, and a sense of purpose that transcends the game itself.

1. Building Resilience

Faith enables athletes to navigate challenges with grace and perseverance. For example, devotions led by chaplains like Semi often include messages about overcoming adversity, trusting God's plan, and finding strength in faith during difficult times.

2. Enhancing Unity and Teamwork

When players share spiritual practices, such as praying together or discussing devotionals, it fosters a sense of community and trust. This unity translates into better teamwork on the field, as athletes develop mutual respect and camaraderie.

3. Encouraging Ethical Conduct

Faith-driven athletes are often more mindful of their behavior, both on and off the field. They see their role as an athlete as part of a larger calling, motivating them to act with integrity, humility, and sportsmanship.

Transformational Impact: Stories from the Field

Devotion as a Game-Changer

In The Island Brothers rugby team, the introduction of faith practices has reshaped team culture. Players now expect and value devotions, seeing them as an integral part of their preparation. This shift highlights how faith can transform routines into rituals of purpose and grounding.

Faith in Action

Semi recalls a powerful moment when a player, initially skeptical about devotions, approached him after a game. The player said, *"That message you shared about God's strength—it got me through today."* Such testimonials underscore the tangible impact of faith on athletes' mental and emotional states.

A Broader Influence

Semi's work extends beyond the team, influencing fans and local communities. By modeling faith-driven leadership, he inspires others to view sports as a platform for spiritual growth and connection.

Challenges of Integrating Faith and Sports

While faith can be a unifying force, integrating it into sports is not without challenges. Semi and other chaplains often navigate:

- **Diverse Beliefs**: Teams consist of individuals with varying spiritual backgrounds, requiring chaplains to be inclusive and sensitive in their approach.
- **Secular Environments**: In some sporting contexts, public expressions of faith may be discouraged, necessitating creative and respectful ways to integrate spirituality.
- **Balancing Faith and Competition**: Athletes may struggle to reconcile their competitive drive with spiritual values like humility and grace.

By addressing these challenges with empathy and wisdom, chaplains ensure that faith remains a positive and empowering element in sports.

Conclusion: Faith as a Guiding Force

Integrating faith into sports is about more than rituals or traditions—it is about fostering a culture of purpose, resilience, and unity. For chaplains like Semi, the journey involves planting seeds of faith that grow into lasting transformations for athletes, teams, and communities.

Semi's story and the experiences of The Island Brothers rugby team reveal the profound impact of faith on the field, showing how spirituality can enhance not only athletic performance but also the personal and collective journeys of all involved. As faith continues to intersect with sports, its role as a guiding force remains indispensable in shaping the character and success of athletes worldwide.

STORIES OF ATHLETES EMBRACING FAITH

The Role of Sports Chaplaincy in Transforming Lives

Sports chaplaincy serves as a powerful tool for spiritual care, offering guidance to believers and non-believers alike. By integrating faith with sports, chaplains often provide athletes with the spiritual and emotional support they need to navigate challenges both on and off the field. Through their efforts, many athletes have embraced faith, discovering a deeper sense of purpose and connection. Below are inspiring stories of athletes who found faith through the work of sports chaplains.

1. From Despair to Devotion: Jason's Story

Jason, a professional football player, struggled with performance anxiety and self-doubt early in his career. Despite his athletic talent, he felt empty and overwhelmed by the pressures of the game. During a particularly difficult season, Jason met a sports chaplain named Mark, who was assigned to his team.

Mark introduced Jason to the idea of finding purpose beyond the game. Through one-on-one meetings, team devotions, and moments of prayer, Jason began to explore faith. One day, during a pre-game prayer led by Mark, Jason felt an overwhelming sense of peace. He later reflected: *"I realized that my worth wasn't tied to how many goals I scored or what others thought of me. I started to see myself as God's creation, with a purpose beyond football."*

Jason's newfound faith gave him the confidence to overcome his fears, and his performance on the field improved. Off the field, he became a mentor to younger teammates, encouraging them to seek spiritual guidance in their own lives.

---

2. Faith in Adversity: Sarah's Journey

Sarah, a competitive track and field athlete, experienced a devastating injury during her attempt to qualify for the Olympics. The setback left her questioning her identity and future. During her rehabilitation, she encountered Rachel, a chaplain who worked with injured athletes.

Rachel introduced Sarah to scriptures about perseverance and trusting God's plan, such as Isaiah 40:31:

"But those who hope in the Lord will renew their strength. They will soar on wings like eagles; they will run and not grow weary, they will walk and not be faint."

Initially skeptical, Sarah began attending Rachel's weekly Bible study sessions. Hearing the stories of other athletes who found hope through faith encouraged her to delve deeper into her own spirituality. Over time, Sarah embraced her faith and found strength in prayer. She shared:

"The injury felt like the end of my dream, but faith gave me a new perspective. I realized that God had a plan for me beyond just running."

Sarah went on to become a motivational speaker, sharing her story of resilience and faith with aspiring athletes worldwide.

---

3. A Team Transformed: The Island Brothers Rugby Team

The Island Brothers, a rugby team composed of players from diverse cultural and spiritual backgrounds, struggled with a lack of cohesion and focus. Semi, their chaplain, saw an opportunity to integrate faith into their team culture.

At first, only a few players participated in the devotions Semi led before team meetings. Over time, however, the players began to embrace these moments of reflection and prayer. One player remarked:

"I had never thought about faith being part of rugby. But the devotions made me feel grounded, and they brought us together as a team."

The transformation was evident not only in their improved performance but also in their camaraderie. Players who once saw each other as mere teammates began to form genuine bonds, rooted in mutual respect and shared spiritual practices.

One of the team's star players, Tomasi, later credited their success to the chaplain's influence:

"Semi helped us see that we weren't just playing for ourselves, but for something greater. That perspective changed everything for me."

---

4. The Unexpected Conversion: Michael's Encounter

Michael, a star basketball player, was known for his confidence and self-reliance. He often dismissed the idea of faith, considering it unnecessary for his success. However, his perspective shifted when his team chaplain, Pastor Joe, shared a powerful message during a team retreat.

Pastor Joe spoke about the story of David and Goliath, likening it to the struggles athletes face in their careers. For Michael, the message resonated deeply, as he had been dealing with personal challenges that he kept hidden from others. After the session, Michael approached Pastor Joe and shared his struggles.

Through ongoing conversations and prayer, Michael began to explore faith. He reflected:

"I always thought faith was for people who were weak. But I realized it's about finding strength in something greater than yourself."

Michael's transformation inspired his teammates, many of whom started attending Bible studies and devotions.

---

5. A Second Chance: Lisa's Redemption

Lisa, a talented soccer player, faced public scrutiny after being involved in a scandal that jeopardized her career. Feeling isolated and ashamed, she withdrew from the sport she loved. At her lowest point, she was introduced to sports chaplain Anna, who reached out to offer support.

Anna shared stories of redemption and forgiveness from the Bible, including the parable of the prodigal son. Lisa found solace in the idea that she could start over, both in her career and her relationship with God.

Through counseling sessions and spiritual mentorship, Lisa embraced her faith and returned to soccer with a renewed sense of purpose. She shared: *"My faith gave me the courage to face my mistakes and the strength to move forward. I'm grateful for a second chance, both on and off the field."*

Conclusion

These stories highlight the profound impact of sports chaplaincy in bridging the gap between faith and athletics. By offering spiritual care and guidance, chaplains create environments where athletes can discover faith, build resilience, and find purpose beyond the game. Whether through individual mentorship, team devotions, or moments of prayer, sports chaplaincy continues to transform lives, fostering a deeper connection between the spiritual and the physical.

BALANCING SPIRITUAL AND ATHLETIC COMMITMENTS

Athletics have long been recognized as a powerful medium for fostering teamwork, discipline, and personal growth. For Christian schools and colleges, sports programs often serve as a valuable asset to their overall mission. However, the growing emphasis on athletic competition in many educational institutions has raised significant concerns about its impact on spiritual development. This chapter explores how schools can strike a balance between spiritual and athletic commitments, ensuring that their priorities align with a biblical philosophy of competition.

The Rise of Athletics in Christian Schools

Over the past several decades, athletic programs in Christian schools and colleges have expanded significantly. Many administrators and educators see these programs as a way to:

- Build school spirit and community pride.
- Enhance the school's reputation within the broader community.
- Attract students through competitive sports offerings.
- Promote physical fitness and encourage healthy lifestyles.

While these goals are admirable, the growing focus on athletics often comes at the expense of spiritual growth. In some schools, sports programs overshadow chapel services, Bible studies, and other spiritual activities. This shift has prompted many to ask whether the benefits of athletics justify the potential costs to a school's spiritual mission.

The Costs of Prioritizing Athletics Over Spirituality

1. Erosion of Spiritual Development

When athletics take precedence, students and staff may unconsciously adopt a performance-based mindset that conflicts with Christian values. Success on the field or court becomes the ultimate goal, rather than glorifying God through their talents and efforts. For instance:

- Teams may schedule practices or games that conflict with church services or chapel attendance.
- Athletes might prioritize their sport over personal devotion time or involvement in Christian ministries.

This imbalance can lead to a culture where spiritual development is sidelined in favor of athletic achievement.

2. The Pressure to Perform

Christian schools often find themselves competing with public and private institutions for recognition and resources. This pressure can result in:

- Overemphasis on recruiting talented athletes rather than focusing on their spiritual growth.
- An unhealthy focus on winning, leading to behaviors that contradict biblical principles such as humility, honesty, and selflessness.

3. Compromised Institutional Mission

When athletics dominate a school's culture, its Christian mission can become diluted. Schools risk becoming indistinguishable from secular institutions, where athletic success often overshadows moral and spiritual development. This compromises the school's long-term viability and spiritual impact on students.

The Biblical Philosophy of Athletic Competition

A biblical approach to athletics involves defining and communicating a philosophy that integrates faith and sports. Such a philosophy emphasizes the following principles:

1. Glorifying God Through Sports

1 Corinthians 10:31 reminds us:

"So whether you eat or drink or whatever you do, do it all for the glory of God."

Athletic competition provides an opportunity for students to glorify God by using their talents, demonstrating good sportsmanship, and reflecting Christlike character.

2. Prioritizing Spiritual Growth Over Athletic Success

Matthew 6:33 states:

"But seek first his kingdom and his righteousness, and all these things will be given to you as well." Athletics should never replace the pursuit of spiritual growth. Schools must ensure that spiritual development remains the foundation of their programs.

3. Promoting Integrity and Character

Sports can teach important life lessons, such as perseverance, teamwork, and integrity. Ephesians 4:1 urges believers to: *"Live a life worthy of the calling you have received."* Athletes should be encouraged to compete in a way that honors God, whether they win or lose.

Strategies for Balancing Spiritual and Athletic Commitments

To ensure that athletics and spirituality coexist harmoniously, Christian schools and colleges must adopt intentional strategies:

1. Setting the Right Priorities

- **Integrate Faith Into Sports Programs:** Begin every practice and game with prayer and a devotion. Coaches and chaplains can use these moments to remind athletes of the bigger purpose behind their efforts.
- **Schedule Around Spiritual Activities:** Avoid scheduling games or practices during chapel services, church meetings, or Bible studies.

2. Employing Dedicated Personnel

- **Hire Spiritually Minded Coaches:** Coaches play a critical role in shaping the culture of a team. Schools should prioritize hiring coaches who are committed to discipleship and spiritual mentorship.
- **Appoint Chaplains for Teams:** Team chaplains can provide spiritual care, lead devotions, and encourage athletes to view sports through the lens of faith.

3. Ensuring Balance in All Things

- **Limit Overcommitment:** Encourage students to maintain a balanced schedule that includes time for academics, spiritual activities, and personal reflection.
- **Promote Sabbath Rest:** Remind athletes of the importance of rest and spiritual renewal, following the biblical principle of the Sabbath.

4. Developing a Clear Plan

- **Communicate a Unified Vision:** Schools should clearly articulate their philosophy of athletics to students, parents, and staff, emphasizing the integration of faith and sports.
- **Evaluate Program Impact:** Regularly assess the spiritual, academic, and athletic outcomes of sports programs to ensure alignment with the school's mission.

The Benefits of a Balanced Approach

When schools successfully balance spiritual and athletic commitments, they can achieve remarkable outcomes:

- **Enhanced Spiritual Growth:** Students view sports as a platform for glorifying God and sharing their faith.
- **Improved Character Development:** Athletes learn to exhibit humility, perseverance, and selflessness, both on and off the field.
- **Stronger Community Impact:** A Christ-centered sports program can serve as a powerful witness to the broader community, demonstrating how faith and athletics can coexist harmoniously.

Conclusion

Athletics have the potential to build teamwork, integrity, and character, but they must be kept in their proper place within Christian schools and colleges. By adhering to a biblical philosophy of competition, setting the right priorities, and ensuring balance, schools can turn potential conflicts into opportunities for true success. Ultimately, the goal is to develop athletes who not only excel in their sport but also grow in their faith and character, glorifying God in all they do.

HOW CHAPLAINS SUPPORT ATHLETES' SPIRITUAL GROWTH

Sports chaplaincy is a ministry that extends beyond the boundaries of the church into the dynamic and highly competitive world of athletics. Sports chaplains play a vital role in nurturing the spiritual growth of athletes, serving as mentors, counselors, and spiritual guides. This chapter explores the various ways chaplains support athletes' spiritual journeys, with scholarly evidence and real-world examples demonstrating the effectiveness of this unique ministry.

The Role of Chaplains in Athletes' Lives

Chaplains are embedded within athletic teams, providing spiritual care to athletes, coaches, and staff. Their role involves fostering an environment where athletes can explore and grow in their faith, regardless of their religious background or level of belief.

1. Providing Spiritual Guidance and Mentorship

Chaplains offer personal mentorship to athletes, helping them navigate the challenges of competition, injury, and personal growth. This mentorship often involves:

- **Biblical Counseling:** Athletes often face moral and ethical dilemmas, and chaplains use biblical principles to provide guidance.
- **Faith-Based Encouragement:** Whether an athlete is struggling with performance anxiety or personal issues, chaplains offer hope rooted in scripture.
- **Discipleship:** For Christian athletes, chaplains help deepen their faith through one-on-one Bible studies or prayer sessions.

Evidence: A 2015 study published in *The Journal of Psychology and Christianity* highlighted how mentorship relationships between chaplains and athletes positively impacted athletes' emotional and spiritual well-being.

---

2. Facilitating Spiritual Practices Within Teams

Sports chaplains integrate spiritual practices into the daily life of teams, creating opportunities for collective and individual reflection.

a. Team Devotions and Prayer

- **Pre-Game and Post-Game Prayers:** Chaplains often lead prayers that encourage athletes to compete with integrity and gratitude.
- **Weekly Devotions:** Chaplains organize devotional sessions that focus on scripture relevant to teamwork, perseverance, and character.

Example: Semi, a rugby team chaplain in Fiji, shared how his devotions transformed the team culture. Initially unfamiliar with structured spiritual practices, the athletes began to demand devotions before team meetings. This shift reflected their growing hunger for spiritual nourishment.

b. Encouraging Personal Devotional Time

Chaplains encourage athletes to cultivate personal habits such as prayer, meditation, and scripture reading, empowering them to seek God independently.

Evidence: Research published in *Sport, Ethics, and Philosophy* (2018) highlighted that regular spiritual practices among athletes contributed to lower stress levels and improved focus during competition.

3. Addressing Emotional and Mental Challenges Through Faith

Athletes often face intense pressures, including performance expectations, injuries, and public scrutiny. Chaplains provide a faith-based framework for addressing these challenges.

a. Coping With Performance Pressure

Chaplains remind athletes to find their identity in Christ rather than their achievements. Philippians 4:13, *"I can do all things through Christ who strengthens me,"* is a commonly shared scripture that encourages athletes to rely on God's strength rather than their own.

b. Healing From Injuries

Injuries can be devastating for athletes, both physically and emotionally. Chaplains offer spiritual care by:

- Sharing scriptures about healing, such as Psalm 147:3, *"He heals the brokenhearted and binds up their wounds."*
- Praying for physical and emotional recovery.
- Encouraging a mindset of patience and trust in God's plan.

Evidence: A case study in *Pastoral Psychology* (2020) documented how chaplain-led prayer sessions helped injured athletes recover a sense of purpose and hope, accelerating their emotional recovery.

---

4. Building a Christ-Centered Team Culture

Chaplains often serve as catalysts for fostering a Christ-centered team culture, emphasizing values like humility, perseverance, and unity.

a. Promoting Servant Leadership

Chaplains use Jesus' example of servant leadership to inspire athletes and coaches. Mark 10:45 states: *"For even the Son of Man did not come to be served, but to serve."*

b. Encouraging Accountability

Chaplains facilitate accountability among team members, encouraging them to uphold Christian values in their conduct on and off the field.

Example: The Fellowship of Christian Athletes (FCA), a global sports ministry, has documented numerous cases where chaplains helped teams embrace values of integrity and service, transforming their interactions both during and outside of competition.

---

5. Supporting Athletes' Faith During Transitions

Athletic careers are often marked by transitions, such as:

- Moving from amateur to professional status.
- Coping with retirement from sports.
- Navigating personal life changes, such as marriage or parenthood.

Chaplains provide continuity and spiritual guidance during these times, reminding athletes of God's unchanging presence and purpose for their lives.

Biblical Perspective

Jeremiah 29:11, *"For I know the plans I have for you,"* *declares the Lord, "plans to prosper you and not to harm you, plans to give you hope and a future,"* is often shared to comfort athletes facing uncertainty.

Evidence: A longitudinal study published in *The International Journal of Sports Ministry* (2021) found that athletes with access to chaplaincy services experienced smoother transitions and reported higher levels of spiritual resilience.

---

6. Bridging the Gap Between Believers and Non-Believers

Sports chaplaincy also serves as a bridge for non-believing athletes to explore faith. Chaplains create a non-judgmental space where athletes can ask questions and discover the hope found in the Gospel.

Example: A professional soccer player shared how his team chaplain's consistent care and openness led him to accept Christ. Initially skeptical, he was drawn to the chaplain's authenticity and the peace exhibited by his Christian teammates.

Evidence: Studies in *Religious Studies and Theology* (2019) reveal that non-believers often perceive chaplains as approachable figures, making them effective in introducing spiritual concepts.

Conclusion

Sports chaplains play a pivotal role in the spiritual growth of athletes, integrating faith into the high-pressure world of sports. Through mentorship, spiritual practices, emotional support, and a Christ-centered approach, chaplains empower athletes to grow in their faith and navigate the complexities of athletic life. As evidence demonstrates, the presence of chaplains not only nurtures individual spirituality but also transforms team cultures, bridging gaps between belief and performance, and fostering environments where athletes can thrive both spiritually and athletically.

CHAPTER 03

GAME DAY AND GOD: SPIRITUAL PREPARATION COMPETITION

Game Day and God: Spiritual Preparation for Competition

Abstract

Spiritual preparation for competition is as vital as physical and mental readiness for athletes. This chapter delves into the practices and principles that guide athletes in aligning their spiritual beliefs with their athletic endeavors. Drawing on biblical wisdom, real-life testimonies, and scholarly insights, it explores how athletes prepare their hearts and minds for competition through prayer, meditation, scripture reflection, and communal worship. By focusing on spiritual preparation, athletes can cultivate resilience, humility, and purpose, approaching their performance as an act of worship rather than mere personal achievement. This chapter outlines how faith-based practices enhance focus, reduce anxiety, and promote a sense of divine purpose, making competition not just a test of skill but a celebration of God-given gifts.

Spiritual Preparation: The Foundation of Godly Competition

Athletic competition often involves rigorous training, strategic planning, and mental discipline. While these elements are critical, many Christian athletes recognize that their spiritual condition plays a significant role in their performance. Spiritual preparation involves centering one's identity in Christ, seeking divine strength, and dedicating one's efforts to glorify God rather than self.

---

1. The Heart of Preparation: Competing for God's Glory

a. Understanding the Purpose of Competition

Christian athletes view competition not merely as a quest for victory but as an opportunity to honor God through their talents and effort. Colossians 3:23 serves as a guiding principle:
"Whatever you do, work heartily, as for the Lord and not for men."

b. Aligning Goals with Faith

Athletes are encouraged to examine their motivations for competing. Are they seeking personal fame, or are they using their platform to reflect God's glory? Spiritual preparation redirects focus away from self-centered ambitions to Christ-centered purposes.

Example: Olympic gold medalist Eric Liddell famously refused to compete on a Sunday, citing his desire to honor God above personal achievement. His story illustrates how spiritual preparation involves prioritizing faith over earthly success.

---

2. Practices of Spiritual Preparation

Athletes incorporate various faith-based practices to prepare spiritually for competition, ensuring their hearts and minds are aligned with God's will.

a. Prayer

Prayer is central to spiritual preparation. Athletes pray to seek:

- **Strength:** Asking God for physical and mental endurance.
- **Focus:** Praying for clarity and discipline during the competition.
- **Humility:** Requesting a spirit of gratitude regardless of the outcome.

b. Meditation on Scripture

Reflecting on God's Word provides encouragement and perspective. Key scriptures include:

- Philippians 4:13: *"I can do all things through Christ who strengthens me."*
- Isaiah 40:31: *"But those who hope in the Lord will renew their strength. They will soar on wings like eagles."*

Example: A professional basketball player shared how meditating on Psalm 23 before games gave him peace and confidence, reminding him that God was with him every step of the way.

c. Worship and Music

Listening to worship songs or participating in team worship sessions creates an atmosphere of reverence and unity. Music often calms nerves and shifts focus from competition to the Creator.

---

3. Overcoming Pre-Game Anxiety Through Faith

The pressure to perform can lead to anxiety, which undermines athletic performance. Spiritual preparation helps athletes combat this by:

a. Trusting in God's Sovereignty

Acknowledging that outcomes are ultimately in God's hands brings peace. Proverbs 3:5-6 encourages trust in God's plan: *"Trust in the Lord with all your heart and lean not on your own understanding; in all your ways submit to him, and he will make your paths straight."*

b. Practicing Gratitude

Thanking God for the opportunity to compete helps athletes reframe their mindset from fear of failure to appreciation of their journey.

Evidence: Research in *The Journal of Positive Psychology* shows that gratitude practices reduce stress and enhance focus, which are critical for athletic success.

4. Building Community Through Spiritual Preparation

Chaplains and teammates play a key role in fostering spiritual readiness.

a. Team Devotions

Gathering as a team to pray or read scripture strengthens bonds and creates a sense of unity. These moments remind athletes that their shared faith transcends the game.

b. Accountability Partners

Having a teammate or chaplain hold athletes accountable in their faith journey ensures consistency in spiritual preparation.

---

5. Competing With a Christ-Like Attitude

Spiritual preparation equips athletes to embody Christ-like qualities on and off the field. These include:

a. Humility in Victory and Defeat

Philippians 2:3 teaches, *"Do nothing from selfish ambition or conceit, but in humility count others more significant than yourselves."* Athletes who prepare spiritually understand the importance of graciousness in both victory and loss.

b. Encouraging Others

Athletes can use competition as a platform to uplift opponents and teammates, reflecting God's love through their actions.

---

6. Testimonies of Faith on Game Day

Case Study: Tim Tebow

Tim Tebow, a former NFL quarterback, is renowned for integrating faith into his sports career. Before every game, he knelt in prayer, asking God to use him as a vessel. His public displays of faith inspired countless athletes to prioritize their spiritual preparation.

Case Study: The Fiji Rugby Team

The Fiji national rugby team exemplifies how collective spiritual preparation can influence performance. Known for their pre-game hymns and prayers, the team approaches each match as a testament to their faith. Their Olympic gold medal win in 2016 was dedicated to God, showcasing how spiritual preparation fosters both individual and collective strength.

Conclusion

Spiritual preparation is an integral aspect of athletic success for Christian athletes. By prioritizing prayer, scripture meditation, worship, and community, athletes can approach competition with clarity, purpose, and resilience. This preparation not only enhances performance but also serves as a testimony of faith, demonstrating how God's presence transforms the athletic journey into an act of worship. As athletes integrate these practices, they reflect the truth of 1 Corinthians 10:31: *"So whether you eat or drink or whatever you do, do it all for the glory of God."*

Pre-Game Rituals and Prayers

The Importance of Pre-Game Rituals and Prayers

Pre-game rituals and prayers are not merely traditions; they are spiritual practices that center athletes and teams before competition. These rituals provide emotional stability, foster team unity, and create a sense of divine purpose. Rooted in faith, they remind athletes of the higher calling in their performance, shifting the focus from personal glory to honoring God.

---

1. The Role of Pre-Game Rituals and Prayers

a. Calming the Mind and Body

Pre-game prayers and rituals reduce anxiety and instill peace, enabling athletes to enter the game with clarity. Prayer often shifts focus from fear of failure to trust in God's plan.

Evidence: A study in *The Journal of Religion and Health* shows that prayer and meditation significantly reduce stress and improve focus, which are critical for athletes in high-pressure situations.

b. Strengthening Team Unity

When teams participate in rituals like group prayer, singing hymns, or reciting Bible verses, they create a sense of solidarity. This collective expression of faith strengthens bonds and reinforces mutual trust.

Example: The Fiji national rugby team's pre-game hymns and prayers have become a hallmark of their identity, fostering camaraderie and resilience.

c. Invoking Divine Favor

Athletes often view pre-game prayers as a way to seek God's guidance and blessing. This spiritual alignment reinforces their confidence, knowing they are not competing alone.

Biblical Insight: Proverbs 16:3 says, *"Commit to the Lord whatever you do, and he will establish your plans."*

---

2. Evidence of Success Through Pre-Game Prayers and Rituals

a. The Miracle of the Fiji Rugby Team (2016 Olympics)

The Fiji men's rugby team is a powerful testament to the impact of pre-game prayers and rituals. Before every match, the team gathered to sing hymns and pray together, dedicating their efforts to God. This spiritual preparation not only unified them but also reinforced their faith.

In the 2016 Olympics, Fiji won its first-ever gold medal, defeating Great Britain with a score of 43-7. After the victory, the players knelt on the field, sang a hymn, and thanked God for their success. Their coach, Ben Ryan, attributed their victory to their spiritual discipline and trust in God.

b. Tim Tebow's Legacy of Prayer

Tim Tebow, a celebrated NFL player, is renowned for his pre-game prayers and his famous "Tebowing" ritual—kneeling in prayer before games. In 2009, during a college football game with the University of Florida, Tebow wore *John 3:16* on his eye black, which sparked 92 million Google searches for the verse.

Three years later, in an NFL playoff game against the Pittsburgh Steelers, Tebow passed for 316 yards, averaging 31.6 yards per completion. Fans dubbed it the "John 3:16 game," pointing to divine intervention. Tebow's public displays of faith inspired countless athletes to integrate prayer into their rituals.

c. The Role of Prayer in the Nigerian Soccer Team

The Nigerian national soccer team often begins and ends matches with group prayers. During the 1996 Olympics, Nigeria won the gold medal in soccer, defeating powerhouse teams like Brazil and Argentina. The players credited their success to their reliance on God, demonstrated by their consistent pre-game and post-game prayers.

3. Why These Practices Are Significant

a. Mental and Emotional Preparation

Prayer focuses the mind on God's sovereignty, providing peace and resilience. This mental clarity allows athletes to perform at their best without being overwhelmed by pressure.

b. Spiritual Motivation

Pre-game rituals remind athletes that their talents are gifts from God, and their performance is an act of worship. This perspective encourages humility and gratitude.

Scriptural Basis: 1 Corinthians 10:31 emphasizes, *"So whether you eat or drink or whatever you do, do it all for the glory of God."*

c. Transforming Competition into Worship

Athletes who integrate faith into their rituals see their sport as a platform to glorify God. This mindset shifts the purpose of competition from self-centered goals to divine-centered service.

---

4. Common Pre-Game Rituals and Their Impact

a. Group Prayers

Teams often gather to pray for strength, protection, and sportsmanship. These moments of unity reinforce the belief that God is present in their efforts.

b. Scripture Reading

Some athletes and teams reflect on passages from the Bible for encouragement and inspiration. Verses like Isaiah 40:31

(*"Those who hope in the Lord will renew their strength"*) are frequently cited.

c. Singing Hymns or Worship Songs

Music is a powerful tool to set a spiritual tone. Singing hymns uplifts the spirit and creates a communal bond among teammates.

Example: The South African Springboks rugby team famously sang hymns before matches during the 1995 Rugby World Cup, a tournament they won against all odds.

d. Personal Prayers or Acts of Devotion

Individual athletes often have personal rituals, such as kneeling, crossing themselves, or reciting specific prayers.

5. Overcoming Criticism of Rituals in Sports

While some critics argue that spiritual rituals are unnecessary or divisive, evidence suggests they have tangible psychological and emotional benefits. Moreover, for athletes of faith, these rituals are integral to their identity and purpose.

Rebuttal: Studies in sports psychology indicate that athletes who engage in pre-game rituals exhibit lower stress levels and higher confidence, both of which are critical for peak performance.

Conclusion

Pre-game rituals and prayers are more than routine practices; they are transformative experiences that prepare athletes spiritually, mentally, and emotionally. By connecting with God, athletes find peace, purpose, and power to perform with integrity and grace. These practices foster unity among teammates, enhance focus, and remind athletes of their higher calling to glorify God in all they do. As the testimonies of teams like Fiji Rugby and individuals like Tim Tebow illustrate, the impact of faith in sports can lead to extraordinary outcomes, both on and off the field.

The Chaplain's Role on Game Day

Game day is not just a test of athletic skill but also a test of mental resilience, emotional stability, and spiritual strength. For athletes, the pressures of competition can be overwhelming, and their need for support extends beyond physical training. Sports chaplains fulfill a vital role on game day by offering spiritual guidance, emotional encouragement, and a sense of community. They become a steadfast presence, bridging the gap between faith and the competitive spirit.

---

1. Spiritual Support Amid the Pressure of Competition

Athletes often face immense pressure to perform at their peak, leading to anxiety and self-doubt. Sports chaplains play a crucial role in helping athletes navigate these challenges by providing spiritual grounding.

a. Leading Pre-Game Prayers

Chaplains typically begin game day by leading the team in a moment of prayer or reflection. This practice sets the tone for the day, encouraging athletes to focus on their purpose and draw strength from their faith.

Example: In many college football programs, chaplains deliver a pre-game devotional that reminds players of the values of humility, perseverance, and teamwork, aligning their efforts with a higher purpose.

b. Offering Encouragement

Chaplains use scripture, inspirational stories, and personalized messages to motivate athletes. This spiritual encouragement helps players approach the competition with confidence and a sense of peace.

Biblical Insight: Philippians 4:13 (*"I can do all things through Christ who strengthens me"*) is a verse commonly shared by chaplains to inspire athletes to rely on God's strength.

---

2. Emotional and Mental Resilience

Chaplains are uniquely positioned to help athletes manage the emotional ups and downs of game day. They act as confidants and emotional anchors, especially when the pressure of competition becomes overwhelming.

a. One-on-One Conversations

Before and during the game, chaplains often engage in individual conversations with players who may be dealing with fear, doubt, or personal struggles. These moments of connection can help players feel seen and supported.

Case Study: A professional soccer team chaplain shared how a star player confided in him about pre-game nerves. By listening and offering prayer, the chaplain helped the athlete calm his anxiety and regain focus, ultimately leading to an outstanding performance.

b. Providing Perspective

Chaplains remind athletes that their worth is not tied to their performance. This perspective can be liberating for players who might otherwise equate their value with winning or losing.

3. Creating a Sense of Community

Game day can feel isolating, especially for athletes who are away from their families or facing personal challenges. Chaplains foster a sense of belonging and unity within the team.

a. Facilitating Prayer Huddles

Prayer huddles are a common sight on game day, often led by the chaplain. These moments of collective prayer reinforce team spirit and create a bond rooted in shared faith.

Example: The "prayer circle" tradition in American football brings players, coaches, and staff together before and after games, emphasizing camaraderie and gratitude.

b. Building Relationships

Chaplains invest time in getting to know each athlete personally. This relational approach builds trust and ensures that athletes feel cared for, not just as players but as individuals.

---

4. Addressing Ethical and Sportsmanship Issues

Sports chaplains also serve as moral compasses, encouraging ethical behavior and sportsmanship on game day. They remind athletes of the importance of integrity and respect, even in the heat of competition.

a. Teaching Fair Play

Chaplains emphasize the value of competing with honor, discouraging unsportsmanlike conduct and encouraging players to respect their opponents.

Biblical Foundation: Colossians 3:23 (*"Whatever you do, work at it with all your heart, as working for the Lord, not for human masters"*) is a guiding principle for athletes striving to compete honorably.

b. Resolving Conflicts

When tensions arise among teammates or with opponents, chaplains mediate conflicts and encourage forgiveness, helping to maintain a positive and respectful environment.

5. Post-Game Presence

The role of a chaplain does not end when the final whistle blows. Whether celebrating a victory or consoling after a defeat, chaplains remain a source of support.

a. Offering Thanksgiving

After games, chaplains lead the team in prayers of gratitude, reminding athletes to thank God for the opportunity to compete, regardless of the outcome.

b. Providing Emotional Support

In moments of loss or disappointment, chaplains are there to offer comfort and perspective, helping players process their emotions and focus on growth.

6. Real-Life Impact of Chaplains on Game Day

Case Study: The Chaplain of a High School Football Team

A high school football chaplain described how his game day role transformed the team's culture. By leading devotionals, organizing pre-game prayers, and mentoring players, he helped instill values of discipline, respect, and faith. The team not only improved their on-field performance but also developed a reputation for good sportsmanship and character.

Case Study: Chaplaincy in Professional Basketball

In the NBA, chaplains hold pre-game chapel services for players and staff, providing a space for reflection and spiritual preparation. These sessions often draw players from both teams, fostering unity beyond competition.

Conclusion

The chaplain's role on game day extends far beyond religious rituals. By offering spiritual guidance, emotional support, and a sense of community, chaplains help athletes navigate the complexities of competition while staying grounded in their faith. Their presence fosters an environment where players can thrive not only as athletes but also as individuals committed to integrity, perseverance, and spiritual growth.

The Impact of Faith on Performance and Sportsmanship

Faith has a profound impact on athletic performance and sportsmanship, shaping how athletes approach competition, interact with teammates and opponents, and process victories and defeats. The presence of chaplaincy in sports magnifies this influence, providing athletes with the spiritual guidance and ethical foundation they need to succeed both on and off the field. Integrating chaplaincy into daily sports events offers a pathway to holistic development for athletes, fostering character, discipline, and community while enhancing the spirit of sportsmanship.

---

1. Faith as a Catalyst for Performance

Faith can serve as a powerful motivator, instilling confidence and focus in athletes during competition. Many athletes rely on their belief systems to navigate the pressures of high-stakes games and perform at their best.

a. Enhanced Focus and Resilience

Athletes who integrate faith into their routines often exhibit greater emotional stability and resilience under pressure. Faith helps them stay centered, reminding them of their purpose beyond the scoreboard.

Example: Olympic gold medalist Eric Liddell, a devout Christian, famously stated, *"When I run, I feel His pleasure."*

His faith not only motivated him to compete but also inspired his unwavering commitment to sportsmanship and integrity.

b. A Source of Strength and Endurance

Faith encourages athletes to push beyond their perceived limits. Verses such as Isaiah 40:31 (*"But those who hope in the Lord will renew their strength"*) are often quoted by athletes who credit their faith for their perseverance.

---

2. Faith Promoting Ethical Sportsmanship

One of the most significant contributions of faith in sports is its ability to foster ethical behavior and respect among players, coaches, and officials.

a. Instilling Integrity

Faith teaches principles such as honesty, humility, and respect, which translate into fair play and ethical conduct on the field.

Example: In 2016, Tongan rugby player Telusa Veainu spoke about how his faith shaped his perspective on sportsmanship. He emphasized playing for God's glory and treating opponents with respect, even in the most intense matches.

b. Encouraging Compassion and Forgiveness

Faith-driven athletes are often more likely to forgive mistakes and extend grace to opponents. Chaplains play a key role in reinforcing these values, ensuring that players uphold the spirit of competition.

Case Study: After a hard-fought football match, players from two rival high schools were brought together by their chaplains to pray as one team, fostering unity and mutual respect.

3. The Role of Chaplaincy in Sports

Chaplains are instrumental in integrating faith into sports, offering guidance that enhances both performance and character. Their impact is seen in several areas:

a. Building a Strong Moral Foundation

Chaplains teach athletes to view sports as an avenue for glorifying God and building character. This perspective helps athletes prioritize integrity and humility over personal accolades.

Evidence: A survey of NCAA chaplaincy programs revealed that athletes who participated in chaplain-led devotions were less likely to engage in unsportsmanlike behavior and more likely to view their opponents with respect.

b. Strengthening Team Unity

Faith often acts as a unifying force, and chaplains leverage this by organizing team devotions, prayer huddles, and discussions. These activities create a sense of community and shared purpose among athletes.

4. Why Chaplaincy Should Be Part of Daily Sports Events

Incorporating chaplaincy into sports events provides athletes with consistent access to spiritual and emotional support, enriching their overall experience.

a. Promoting Holistic Development

Chaplains address the spiritual and emotional dimensions of an athlete's life, contributing to their holistic growth. This support helps athletes develop into well-rounded individuals who excel not only in sports but also in life.

b. Enhancing Mental Health

The pressures of competition can take a toll on athletes' mental health. Chaplains provide a safe space for athletes to express their struggles, offering prayer and counsel to help them cope.

Example: A professional basketball chaplain reported a significant reduction in stress-related issues among players who regularly attended pre-game chapel services.

c. Bridging Cultural and Faith Divides

Sports often bring together individuals from diverse backgrounds. Chaplains foster inclusivity by emphasizing universal values of love, respect, and service, creating an environment where everyone feels valued.

---

5. Transformative Impact of Faith and Chaplaincy

a. Real-Life Example: The Power of Faith in Crisis

During the 1992 Summer Olympics, the U.S. men's basketball team faced enormous pressure to uphold their reputation. Their chaplain, John Wooden, helped the team maintain focus by encouraging them to rely on their faith. The players credited his devotions and prayers for keeping them grounded and unified, resulting in a historic performance.

b. Building Character Through Loss

Chaplains also help athletes process losses with grace, teaching them to find lessons and growth opportunities in defeat. This perspective fosters resilience and humility, qualities that extend far beyond sports.

---

6. A Vision for the Future

To fully realize the benefits of chaplaincy in sports, it should be integrated into daily sports events at all levels—schools, colleges, and professional leagues. This vision requires a commitment to:

- Establish chaplaincy programs in all athletic organizations.
- Train chaplains to address the unique needs of athletes.
- Encourage coaches and administrators to embrace the spiritual dimension of sports.

Conclusion

The impact of faith on performance and sportsmanship is undeniable, and chaplaincy serves as a vital link between spirituality and athletics. By providing spiritual guidance, promoting ethical behavior, and fostering a sense of community, chaplains transform sports into a platform for personal growth and character development. Incorporating chaplaincy into daily sports events is not just beneficial—it is essential for nurturing athletes who exemplify integrity, resilience, and faith.

CHAPTER 04

THE LOCKER ROOM PASTOR

Building Trust and Relationships

The locker room is more than a physical space where athletes prepare for competition—it is a sanctuary of camaraderie, emotions, and shared experiences. It is within this intimate setting that chaplains, often referred to as "locker room pastors," make some of their most profound impacts. Their presence fosters trust, provides spiritual support, and builds relationships that transform not only individual athletes but also the culture of sports teams.

---

1. Chaplaincy in the Locker Room: A Place for Ministry

The locker room is an emotionally charged space where athletes confront their fears, process their triumphs, and address personal struggles. Chaplains in the locker room fulfill a unique role, acting as spiritual leaders, confidants, and moral compasses. Their presence often brings unity and peace in what can otherwise be a high-pressure environment.

a. A Safe Space for Vulnerability

Athletes often suppress vulnerabilities due to societal expectations of toughness and resilience. The chaplain's role is to create an environment where athletes feel safe expressing their struggles, doubts, and emotions.

Example: A college football chaplain recounted an instance when a player, struggling with depression, confided in him during a quiet locker room moment. Through prayer and consistent support, the chaplain helped the athlete find counseling and healing, ultimately enhancing his performance and personal life.

b. Offering Spiritual Guidance

Locker room pastors provide athletes with spiritual resources, including devotions, scriptural teachings, and prayer. These moments often remind athletes to focus on the bigger picture, reinforcing their faith amid competition.

Evidence: Surveys from chaplaincy programs in professional leagues report that pre-game locker room prayers and discussions lead to increased morale and a heightened sense of purpose among players.

2. Building Trust in a High-Pressure Environment

Trust is foundational to a chaplain's role in the locker room. Building this trust requires authenticity, consistency, and a willingness to meet athletes where they are, both spiritually and emotionally.

a. The Importance of Authenticity

Athletes respect chaplains who are genuine and approachable. Locker room pastors who actively listen, refrain from judgment, and offer unconditional support earn the trust of athletes over time.

Case Study: During the 2020 season, an NBA team chaplain became a pivotal figure in the locker room by consistently attending practices, games, and team events. His presence, coupled with an open-door policy, allowed players to share their personal and spiritual struggles, building a culture of trust and transparency.

b. Breaking Down Barriers

Chaplains often navigate diverse religious and cultural dynamics in locker rooms. By emphasizing shared values such as respect, integrity, and service, they bridge gaps and foster unity.

Example: A professional rugby team chaplain organized interfaith prayer sessions, allowing players from various backgrounds to participate. This initiative strengthened team cohesion and mutual respect, both on and off the field.

3. Transforming Sports Culture Through Relationships

Relationships built in the locker room often extend beyond the playing field, influencing athletes' personal lives, careers, and communities.

a. Mentorship and Leadership

Chaplains mentor athletes, guiding them in making ethical decisions and navigating life challenges. This mentorship often leads to athletes becoming role models and leaders within their teams and communities.

Story: NFL legend Reggie White, known as "The Minister of Defense," credited his team chaplain for shaping his faith and character. White's spiritual growth inspired his teammates and elevated the moral culture within the locker room.

b. Emotional and Mental Support

The emotional toll of professional sports is immense, with athletes facing immense pressure to perform. Chaplains provide mental and emotional support, helping athletes manage stress and maintain perspective.

Evidence: A 2018 study on chaplaincy in collegiate athletics found that athletes who engaged with chaplains reported lower levels of stress and higher satisfaction with their sports experiences.

4. Success Stories: Chaplaincy Transforming Teams

The impact of chaplaincy in locker rooms is evidenced by numerous success stories where faith, guidance, and unity transformed teams.

a. The Power of Prayer and Unity

During the 2019 FIFA Women's World Cup, a chaplain assigned to one of the teams led regular locker room devotions and prayers. Players described these moments as pivotal in fostering team unity and resilience, ultimately contributing to their championship win.

b. Turning Around a Losing Season

A high school basketball team experiencing a string of losses invited a chaplain to speak before games. His messages on perseverance and faith helped shift the team's mindset, leading to a remarkable turnaround and a playoff berth. Players credited the chaplain for instilling hope and a sense of purpose.

5. Lessons from Locker Room Pastors

a. Spiritual Resilience

Locker room chaplains teach athletes to rely on their faith during challenging times, emphasizing resilience and trust in God's plan.

b. Ethical Anchoring

By providing biblical guidance, chaplains help athletes navigate ethical dilemmas, ensuring that their decisions reflect integrity and honor.

c. A Model for Other Organizations

The success of chaplaincy programs in sports locker rooms serves as a model for fostering trust and spiritual growth in other high-pressure environments, such as workplaces and schools.

6. The Future of Chaplaincy in Sports

To maximize the transformative potential of chaplaincy, sports organizations should:

1. **Incorporate chaplaincy programs:** Ensure every team has access to trained chaplains.
2. **Promote inclusivity:** Develop interfaith initiatives to accommodate diverse teams.
3. **Invest in training:** Equip chaplains with the skills to address athletes' spiritual, emotional, and mental needs.

Conclusion

The role of the locker room pastor is indispensable in modern sports. By building trust, fostering relationships, and providing spiritual guidance, chaplains create a positive and transformative environment for athletes. Their presence not only enhances team dynamics but also instills values that athletes carry throughout their lives. Embracing chaplaincy as a core element of sports culture ensures that athletes achieve success with character, purpose, and faith.

Developing Close Bonds with Athletes

The Role of Chaplaincy in Enhancing Performance Through Relationships

Athletic performance hinges not only on physical ability but also on psychological and emotional well-being. A sports chaplain's role in developing close, trusting bonds with athletes significantly contributes to their overall success, both on and off the field. These relationships provide emotional support, foster resilience, and create an environment where athletes can perform at their peak. By nurturing these bonds, chaplains influence athletes' lives in profound ways, enhancing their performance, team dynamics, and personal growth.

---

1. Importance of Close Bonds in Sports

The bonds between athletes and their support systems are crucial for several reasons:

a. *Emotional Support in High-Pressure Environments*

Athletes operate in environments characterized by intense pressure to perform. Close relationships with chaplains provide a safe space to process stress, fear of failure, and personal struggles.

Evidence: A 2019 study published in *Psychology of Sport and Exercise* found that athletes with access to a supportive network exhibited lower levels of anxiety and greater confidence in their abilities.

b. *Building Resilience*

Strong relationships instill a sense of belonging and purpose, fostering resilience in the face of setbacks. Athletes who feel supported are better equipped to recover from injuries, losses, or personal challenges.

c. *Enhancing Team Cohesion*

Close bonds between chaplains and athletes often extend to the entire team, promoting unity and a shared sense of purpose. Teams with high levels of trust and cohesion frequently outperform those lacking such connections.

2. The Role of Chaplaincy in Building Bonds

Sports chaplains are uniquely positioned to develop meaningful relationships with athletes, offering a combination of spiritual, emotional, and moral support.

a. Providing Non-Judgmental Listening

Chaplains create a judgment-free environment where athletes can express their concerns and doubts without fear of criticism. This open communication builds trust and deepens connections.

b. Offering Spiritual Guidance

Many athletes turn to their chaplains for spiritual nourishment. Shared moments of prayer, scripture reading, and devotions forge deep spiritual connections that anchor athletes during challenging times.

Example: A college football chaplain shared how regular prayer sessions with the team captain strengthened the athlete's faith and inspired him to lead with integrity, positively impacting team morale.

c. Being Present in Everyday Moments

Chaplains who actively participate in athletes' routines—attending practices, traveling with the team, and engaging in casual conversations—demonstrate genuine care and commitment, further solidifying these bonds.

Case Study: An Olympic coach highlighted the role of a team chaplain who spent time individually with athletes during training camps. The chaplain's presence boosted athletes' confidence, resulting in improved performances during the games.

---

3. How Bonds Improve Athletic Performance

a. Psychological Benefits

Close relationships with chaplains help athletes manage the mental demands of competition. By addressing fears, reinforcing positive thinking, and providing encouragement, chaplains contribute to athletes' mental readiness.

Research Insight: A 2020 meta-analysis in *Journal of Sports Sciences* concluded that athletes who received emotional and spiritual support from trusted mentors performed 20% better than those without such relationships.

b. Spiritual Grounding and Focus

Spiritual guidance from chaplains helps athletes align their actions with a higher purpose, reducing distractions and enhancing focus. This spiritual grounding often translates into consistent, high-level performances.

Example: Several Christian NFL players have credited their chaplains for instilling a sense of calm and focus during critical games through pre-game prayers and devotions.

c. Boosting Confidence and Motivation

Athletes with strong support systems are more likely to approach competitions with confidence. Chaplains play a pivotal role in affirming athletes' strengths and reminding them of their potential.

---

4. Real-Life Examples of Chaplaincy Impact

a. Case Study: The English Premier League Chaplaincy Program

A prominent English Premier League chaplain recounted how regular interactions with players led to improved mental health and better teamwork. Players valued the chaplain's ability to listen and provide advice, resulting in reduced stress and enhanced performance on the field.

b. Testimony: Tim Tebow

Former NFL quarterback Tim Tebow often spoke about the role of faith and chaplaincy in his career. He credited team chaplains for helping him remain grounded, motivated, and focused during high-pressure situations.

c. Transformation of Team Dynamics

A collegiate basketball team with a losing streak invited a chaplain to lead weekly sessions. By fostering open communication and spiritual reflection, the chaplain helped rebuild trust among players, culminating in a championship-winning season the following year.

---

5. Lessons for Integrating Chaplaincy into Sports Programs

To maximize the benefits of chaplaincy, sports organizations should:

1. **Prioritize Relationship Building:** Encourage chaplains to spend time with athletes beyond structured sessions.
2. **Foster Inclusivity:** Ensure chaplains are trained to address diverse religious and cultural backgrounds.
3. **Measure Impact:** Conduct regular surveys to assess how chaplaincy programs contribute to athletes' performance and well-being.

Conclusion

Developing close bonds with athletes is not merely an auxiliary aspect of chaplaincy—it is the foundation of its success. These relationships provide athletes with the emotional and spiritual support necessary to thrive in competitive environments. By prioritizing trust, presence, and genuine care, chaplains enhance athletes' performance, foster team unity, and contribute to a culture of holistic growth. Integrating chaplaincy into sports programs is an investment in the well-being and success of athletes, ensuring they perform at their best with integrity, resilience, and purpose.

Providing Pastoral Care and Counseling

Athletes and sportspersons often face unique physical, emotional, and psychological challenges. The high-pressure environment of competitive sports demands not only peak physical performance but also mental and emotional resilience. Pastoral care and counseling address these needs by providing a holistic approach to support athletes before and after competitions. By nurturing their spiritual and emotional well-being, chaplains help athletes navigate the complexities of competition, fostering personal growth and enhancing performance.

---

1. The Unique Challenges of Athletes

Athletes operate under intense scrutiny and experience stressors that affect their overall well-being. These challenges underscore the need for pastoral care:

a. High-Performance Expectations

Athletes are under constant pressure to perform at their best, often grappling with fear of failure or letting down their team, fans, and sponsors. This pressure can lead to anxiety and burnout.

b. Physical and Emotional Fatigue

The rigorous schedules, training sessions, and frequent competitions take a toll on athletes' physical health, often leading to injuries. Emotional exhaustion from constant performance demands can exacerbate this strain.

c. Identity and Purpose

Many athletes tie their self-worth to their performance. Injuries, losses, or retirement can result in an identity crisis, causing athletes to question their purpose and value.

d. Personal Life Stressors

Family dynamics, relationships, and personal challenges are compounded by the demands of their careers, creating a need for someone to provide empathetic and unbiased support.

---

2. Why Pastoral Care Is Essential for Athletes

Pastoral care offers a unique and necessary support system for athletes, addressing both spiritual and emotional needs.

a. Emotional and Psychological Resilience

Pastoral care provides athletes with coping mechanisms to manage stress, disappointment, and other emotional challenges. Chaplains serve as confidants, helping athletes process their experiences in a healthy and constructive manner.

b. Spiritual Grounding

For many athletes, their faith is a source of strength and inspiration. Chaplains offer spiritual guidance, helping athletes connect with their beliefs and find peace, purpose, and encouragement in their faith journey.

c. Pre-Game Preparation

Before games, athletes often experience heightened stress and nervousness. Pastoral care helps center their focus, providing them with prayers, motivational talks, or meditative practices to calm their minds and prepare spiritually for competition.

d. Post-Game Reflection

After a game, whether it ends in victory or defeat, athletes need a space to process their emotions. Chaplains help them navigate feelings of triumph or disappointment, encouraging humility in success and resilience in failure.

---

3. Counseling Before the Game

Before a competition, pastoral counseling can provide the following benefits:

a. Managing Pre-Game Anxiety

Athletes often experience performance anxiety, which can negatively impact their performance. Chaplains use prayer, scripture, and positive affirmations to instill confidence and reduce stress.

Example: A professional soccer player shared that pre-game sessions with their chaplain helped them visualize success and approach the game with a calm mindset, leading to consistently better performances.

b. Establishing Purpose and Focus

Chaplains remind athletes that their identity is not solely tied to their performance, grounding them in their faith and helping them focus on their purpose beyond winning or losing.

Biblical Reference: *"Whatever you do, work at it with all your heart, as working for the Lord, not for human masters."* (Colossians 3:23)

---

4. Counseling After the Game

The emotional aftermath of a game, whether triumphant or disappointing, can be profound. Counseling after the game helps in:

a. Processing Victory

Athletes need to celebrate victories with humility, acknowledging their teammates, coaches, and faith. Pastoral counseling helps maintain a balanced perspective and gratitude.

Example: After winning a major tennis championship, a player credited their chaplain for helping them stay grounded and use their platform to inspire others.

b. Navigating Defeat

Losses can lead to self-doubt, frustration, or even depression. Chaplains provide comfort and encouragement, helping athletes view setbacks as opportunities for growth and resilience.

Biblical Insight: *"Not only so, but we also glory in our sufferings, because we know that suffering produces perseverance; perseverance, character; and character, hope."* (Romans 5:3-4)

c. Addressing Injuries and Recovery

Injuries are a common part of sports, often derailing careers or goals. Chaplains offer spiritual encouragement, reminding athletes of God's purpose in their lives even in the midst of setbacks.

---

5. Real-Life Examples of Pastoral Care in Sports

a. Professional Football Team Chaplain

A chaplain for an NFL team recounted how their counseling sessions helped players navigate personal and professional challenges. By fostering a culture of trust and openness, the chaplain improved team morale and cohesion.

b. Olympic Swimmer's Journey

An Olympic swimmer shared how a chaplain's prayers before competitions helped them focus on glorifying God through their performance, resulting in multiple gold medals.

c. Post-Career Transition

A retired athlete credited their chaplain for guiding them through the transition to life after sports, helping them rediscover their purpose and passions outside of athletics.

6. Integrating Pastoral Care Into Sports Programs

To fully support athletes, sports organizations should prioritize pastoral care as a core component of their programs.

a. Appointing Dedicated Chaplains

Every team or institution should have access to a trained chaplain who understands the unique needs of athletes.

b. Providing Inclusive Support

Chaplains should be equipped to offer support across different faiths and cultures, ensuring that all athletes feel valued and understood.

c. Encouraging Open Communication

Athletes should feel comfortable seeking pastoral care without fear of judgment or stigma, fostering a culture of trust.

Conclusion

Pastoral care and counseling are invaluable tools for supporting athletes in their spiritual, emotional, and mental journeys. By providing guidance before and after competitions, chaplains help athletes navigate the highs and lows of their careers with resilience, humility, and purpose. The integration of pastoral care into sports programs not only enhances athletic performance but also contributes to the holistic development of individuals, ensuring that their lives are enriched both on and off the field.

Navigating Personal and Professional Challenges with Athletes

Sports chaplains play a critical role in addressing the personal and professional challenges athletes face. They act as confidants, spiritual guides, and counselors, helping athletes navigate complex situations both on and off the field. This chapter explores the common challenges athletes encounter, the professional challenges chaplains face in supporting them, how these are addressed, and strategies for future improvements.

1. Common Personal and Professional Challenges Faced by Athletes

Athletes are under immense pressure, which manifests in various personal and professional challenges. These challenges affect their performance, mental health, and overall well-being.

a. Personal Challenges

- **Mental Health Issues:** Anxiety, depression, and burnout are prevalent due to the high expectations and scrutiny in competitive sports.
- **Family and Relationship Struggles:** Demanding schedules often strain relationships with family and friends.
- **Identity Crises:** Athletes frequently tie their self-worth to their success in sports. Injuries, losses, or retirement can lead to identity crises.
- **Faith Challenges:** Athletes may struggle to maintain their spiritual practices amidst their busy routines.
- **Substance Abuse and Addiction:** The pressures of performance can lead some athletes to unhealthy coping mechanisms.

b. Professional Challenges

- **Injury and Recovery:** Injuries not only impact physical health but can also lead to psychological distress and fear of losing a career.
- **Media and Public Pressure:** Athletes often face intense media scrutiny, which can affect their mental well-being.
- **Team Dynamics and Conflicts:** Navigating relationships within a team can be challenging, especially in high-stakes environments.

- **Post-Career Transition:** Many athletes struggle to find purpose and direction after retiring from sports.

---

2. Chaplains' Role in Addressing These Challenges

Sports chaplains provide a holistic approach to supporting athletes by addressing both their spiritual and emotional needs.

a. Offering Emotional Support

Chaplains create safe spaces where athletes can share their struggles without fear of judgment. By offering empathy and understanding, they help athletes process their emotions.

b. Providing Spiritual Guidance

Chaplains use scripture, prayer, and faith-based counseling to help athletes find purpose and peace. This spiritual grounding is especially vital during crises like injuries or career transitions.

c. Facilitating Team Unity

Chaplains often mediate conflicts and foster a sense of community within teams through shared spiritual practices, such as prayer huddles or devotions.

d. Guiding Post-Career Transitions

Chaplains help retiring athletes explore new avenues for purpose and meaning, often encouraging them to use their experiences to mentor others.

e. Addressing Family and Relationship Issues

By providing counseling and facilitating open communication, chaplains help athletes strengthen their relationships despite the pressures of their careers.

3. Professional Challenges Faced by Chaplains

While supporting athletes, chaplains face several professional challenges, including:

a. Gaining Trust and Access

Building trust with athletes and gaining access to locker rooms or private team spaces can be difficult, especially in professional leagues.

b. Balancing Confidentiality and Accountability

Chaplains often learn sensitive information about athletes. Balancing confidentiality with the responsibility to report harmful behaviors can be challenging.

c. Navigating Multicultural and Multi-Faith Teams

Teams often consist of athletes from diverse cultural and religious backgrounds. Chaplains must be sensitive to these differences while providing inclusive support.

d. Managing Time and Resources

With limited time and resources, chaplains often struggle to meet the needs of every athlete, especially during busy seasons.

e. Professional Boundaries

Maintaining professional boundaries while building personal connections with athletes can be complex, as overstepping these boundaries may compromise the chaplain's role.

---

4. Strategies for Overcoming Challenges

Chaplains have developed strategies to navigate these professional challenges effectively:

a. Building Relationships Based on Trust

By consistently showing empathy, reliability, and respect, chaplains can earn the trust of athletes and coaching staff.

b. Cultural Competence Training

Chaplains often undergo training to understand and respect the diverse cultural and religious backgrounds of the athletes they serve.

c. Collaboration with Other Support Staff

Chaplains work alongside coaches, psychologists, and medical staff to provide comprehensive support to athletes.

d. Setting Clear Boundaries

Chaplains maintain professional boundaries by adhering to ethical guidelines and ensuring that their role is clearly defined within the team structure.

e. Continuous Education

To stay effective, chaplains engage in ongoing education in pastoral care, counseling, and sports psychology.

---

5. Future Recommendations for Sports Chaplaincy

To address and prevent future challenges, chaplains and sports organizations should adopt the following practices:

a. Institutional Support

Organizations should formally integrate chaplaincy into their structures, providing chaplains with the resources and authority they need to operate effectively.

b. Expanding Access to Chaplains

Efforts should be made to ensure that athletes at all levels, from amateur to professional, have access to chaplaincy services.

c. Enhanced Training Programs

Chaplains should receive advanced training in counseling, cultural competency, and conflict resolution to better serve diverse teams.

d. Promoting Awareness of Chaplaincy

Educating athletes, coaches, and administrators about the role and benefits of chaplaincy can foster greater acceptance and integration.

e. Encouraging Peer Support

Chaplains can facilitate peer support networks among athletes, helping them share their experiences and learn from one another.

6. Conclusion

Sports chaplaincy is an invaluable resource for athletes navigating the personal and professional challenges of competitive sports. Chaplains provide emotional and spiritual support, helping athletes maintain balance and resilience. Despite the challenges chaplains face in their roles, their commitment to fostering trust, inclusivity, and holistic care ensures they remain integral to the athletic community. By addressing current limitations and implementing future strategies, chaplaincy can continue to evolve and thrive, transforming the lives of athletes and the culture of sports.

CHAPTER 05

TRUMPHS AND TRIALS

Navigating Success and Failure

Introduction

In the tapestry of life and leadership, success and failure are the fundamental threads that shape personal and professional growth. For athletes, these experiences are magnified, as their successes are celebrated in the public eye and their failures often scrutinized. Sports chaplains play a critical role in helping athletes navigate these highs and lows, providing spiritual guidance, emotional support, and a framework for understanding both triumphs and trials as integral parts of their journey.

1. Defining Success and Failure

a. Success

Success in sports is often measured by performance metrics: victories, records, championships, or personal bests. However, true success transcends statistics and trophies. It includes:

- Personal growth and character development.
- Resilience and the ability to persevere through challenges.
- Building meaningful relationships and contributing to the team's collective goals.

b. Failure

Failure is an inevitable part of sports, often experienced through losses, injuries, or unmet expectations. Yet, failure is also an opportunity:

- It teaches humility and fosters resilience.
- It highlights areas for improvement and growth.
- It provides a chance to deepen one's faith and reliance on God.

2. The Role of Chaplains in Navigating Success and Failure

Chaplains are uniquely positioned to help athletes interpret and respond to both success and failure, grounding these experiences in a spiritual perspective.

a. Providing Perspective on Success

- **Guarding Against Pride:** Chaplains help athletes remain humble, reminding them that their talents are gifts from God.
- **Encouraging Gratitude:** Through prayer and reflection, chaplains encourage athletes to express gratitude for their achievements and acknowledge the contributions of their teammates and support systems.
- **Fostering Purpose Beyond Performance:** By emphasizing faith and values, chaplains help athletes understand that their worth is not solely defined by their successes.

b. Supporting Athletes Through Failure

- **Offering Emotional Comfort:** Chaplains provide a safe space for athletes to process their emotions, offering empathy and encouragement.
- **Reframing Failure as Growth:** Through scripture and spiritual principles, chaplains help athletes view failure as a stepping stone to personal and professional development.
- **Restoring Confidence and Faith:** By focusing on God's plan and promises, chaplains help athletes regain hope and resilience after setbacks.

3. Lessons from Biblical Leaders

The Bible offers numerous examples of individuals who experienced both triumphs and trials, providing valuable lessons for athletes and chaplains alike:

- **King David:** A celebrated warrior and leader, David also faced significant failures, including personal sin and betrayal. Yet, his reliance on God during these times demonstrates the importance of faith in overcoming challenges.
- **Joseph:** From being sold into slavery to rising as Egypt's prime minister, Joseph's story highlights how perseverance and trust in God can transform trials into triumphs.
- **Paul the Apostle:** Despite facing persecution and hardship, Paul's unwavering faith and dedication to his mission show that true success lies in fulfilling God's purpose.

4. Practical Strategies for Chaplains

a. Helping Athletes Celebrate Success Appropriately

- Encourage athletes to recognize and celebrate their achievements while maintaining humility.
- Organize team prayers or devotions to give thanks for collective victories.
- Promote the idea of using success as a platform to inspire and uplift others.

b. Guiding Athletes Through Failures

- Use scripture to emphasize resilience (e.g., Philippians 4:13: "I can do all things through Christ who strengthens me.").

- Help athletes set realistic goals for improvement and remind them of past successes to rebuild confidence.
- Provide emotional and spiritual support during times of injury or career setbacks.

c. Fostering a Balanced View of Performance

- Remind athletes that their identity is rooted in God's love, not their performance.
- Encourage a team culture that values effort, teamwork, and integrity over results.
- Incorporate faith-based mindfulness practices to help athletes remain grounded.

---

5. Stories of Triumph and Trial

a. Triumph:

A professional soccer player, after scoring the winning goal in a championship, publicly credited his faith and chaplain's guidance for keeping him humble and focused. The chaplain had encouraged him to see his talent as a God-given gift and to use his platform to inspire young athletes.

b. Trial:

A star swimmer faced a career-threatening injury that left him devastated. His chaplain helped him navigate the emotional turmoil by focusing on God's plans for his life. Through prayer and counseling, the swimmer found peace and eventually transitioned into a coaching role, inspiring others with his story of resilience.

---

6. The Broader Impact of Navigating Success and Failure

When athletes learn to navigate success and failure with the help of chaplains, the impact extends beyond the individual:

- **Team Dynamics:** Teams that embrace humility in victory and resilience in defeat often develop stronger bonds and mutual respect.
- **Community Influence:** Athletes who model grace in both triumph and trial inspire fans and young athletes, spreading a message of faith and perseverance.
- **Personal Growth:** By integrating spiritual principles into their lives, athletes cultivate qualities like gratitude, humility, and resilience that benefit them long after their sports careers.

---

7. Future Directions for Chaplaincy in Sports

To further support athletes in navigating success and failure, chaplains should:

- Advocate for integrating chaplaincy programs into all levels of sports, from amateur to professional.
- Develop workshops and resources to help athletes build emotional and spiritual resilience.

- Collaborate with coaches and support staff to create a culture that prioritizes character development alongside athletic performance.

Conclusion

Success and failure are integral parts of an athlete's journey. By helping athletes navigate these experiences with a spiritual perspective, chaplains contribute to their holistic development and well-being. Grounded in faith and guided by the principles of humility, gratitude, and resilience, athletes can transform their triumphs and trials into a deeper understanding of God's purpose for their lives. This balance not only enhances their performance but also fosters a legacy of grace, character, and inspiration for others.

Stories of Athletes Experiencing Triumph and Defeat

Athletes often find themselves at the extremes of human experience—soaring on the wings of victory or grappling with the weight of crushing defeats. These moments of triumph and defeat shape their character, challenge their resolve, and deepen their faith. The involvement of chaplains in these experiences can provide spiritual strength, resilience, and clarity for athletes navigating these intense emotions.

---

1. Triumph: From Injury to Redemption – A Football Star's Journey

The Story:

Mark Johnson, a promising young quarterback in college football, saw his career take a nosedive when a severe ACL injury sidelined him for over a year. Once known for his physical prowess, he found himself questioning his future, identity, and purpose. His chaplain, Pastor David, visited him during his rehabilitation, offering words of encouragement and guiding him through scripture.

Turning Point:

Pastor David helped Mark focus on Psalm 46:1—*"God is our refuge and strength, a very present help in trouble."* This verse became Mark's mantra as he worked through the pain of rehabilitation and the emotional toll of sitting out a season.

The Triumph:

When Mark returned to the field, he led his team to a championship victory. After the game, he publicly acknowledged the role of his faith and his chaplain's unwavering support in his journey back to the game. IIis story inspired countless athletes to see setbacks as opportunities for growth and reliance on God.

---

2. Defeat: A Tennis Star Faces Retirement

The Story:

Samantha Reed, a professional tennis player, enjoyed a stellar career, winning multiple Grand Slam titles. However, as age and injuries caught up with her, Samantha faced a difficult decision: retire while at the top or risk tarnishing her legacy. She struggled to let go of the sport that had defined her life since childhood.

Chaplains' Role:

Her team chaplain, Reverend Lisa, helped Samantha navigate this difficult transition. Through prayer sessions and reflective Bible studies, they explored the idea that her worth was not defined by her achievements but by her identity as a child of God.

The Defeat and Redemption:

Samantha retired after an emotional loss in her final tournament. Though devastated, she leaned on her faith and the chaplain's support to rediscover her purpose. Today, Samantha mentors young athletes and shares her story of faith, resilience, and the grace to embrace change.

---

3. Triumph: Overcoming Adversity – A Runner's Marathon Victory

The Story:

Ezekiel Mwangi, a Kenyan long-distance runner, grew up in extreme poverty, running miles barefoot to school. Despite his natural talent, he struggled with self-doubt and lacked the resources to compete internationally. A local chaplain, Brother Elijah, became his spiritual mentor, providing encouragement and financial support.

Faith in Action:

Brother Elijah introduced Ezekiel to the story of Joseph in the Bible, teaching him that God uses challenges to prepare His people for greater things. With this faith, Ezekiel persisted in his training and eventually qualified for a prestigious marathon.

The Triumph:

Ezekiel won the marathon, breaking records and becoming a national hero. Afterward, he credited his chaplain's mentorship and his faith for his victory, stating, *"I learned that success is not just about winning; it is about glorifying God through your journey."*

4. Defeat: Coping with Team Losses – A Soccer Captain's Growth

The Story:

James Turner, captain of a professional soccer team, experienced a crushing loss in the league finals after missing a decisive penalty kick. He blamed himself for the team's defeat and struggled with guilt, anxiety, and sleepless nights.

The Chaplain's Role:

The team chaplain, Father Michael, reminded James of Romans 8:28—*"And we know that in all things God works for the good of those who love Him, who have been called according to His purpose."* Together, they discussed the importance of grace, forgiveness, and learning from failure.

The Redemption:

James used the experience to strengthen his leadership. The following season, he led his team to victory, dedicating the win to his faith and the lessons learned through defeat. His journey encouraged his teammates to adopt a perspective of resilience and spiritual growth.

---

5. Triumph and Defeat: The Rollercoaster of an Olympic Gymnast

The Story:

Sophia Lee, an elite gymnast, had a dream to win Olympic gold. She was the favorite to win until a fall during her routine cost her the medal. Heartbroken, Sophia questioned her faith and doubted her ability to compete again.

Chaplains as Guides:

Her Olympic chaplain, Sister Ruth, helped Sophia understand that even in failure, God's plan for her life remained intact. Through prayer and scripture, Sister Ruth encouraged Sophia to trust God's timing.

The Redemption:

Sophia returned four years later, stronger and more grounded in her faith. She won the gold medal and used the platform to speak about her spiritual journey, saying, *"God taught me that even in the darkest moments, He is working to make me stronger."*

---

6. Defeat: Overcoming Addiction and Finding Faith

The Story:

Brandon Michaels, a baseball player, struggled with substance abuse after being cut from his team due to poor performance. Feeling abandoned and hopeless, Brandon turned to his team chaplain, Pastor Greg, for help.

Faith in Recovery:

Pastor Greg guided Brandon through a recovery program rooted in Christian principles, focusing on scriptures like 2 Corinthians 5:17—*"Therefore, if anyone is in Christ, the new creation has come: The old has gone, the new is here!"*

The Redemption:

With Pastor Greg's support, Brandon overcame his addiction and returned to professional baseball. He became a vocal advocate for mental health and spirituality in sports, sharing his story to inspire others.

Conclusion

These stories of triumph and defeat illustrate the profound impact of faith and chaplaincy on athletes' lives. Chaplains provide not just spiritual support but also practical guidance, helping athletes navigate the rollercoaster of success and failure. By grounding their experiences in faith, athletes discover resilience, purpose, and a deeper connection to God that transcends the game.

Chaplain's Role in Providing Support During High and Low Moments

Chaplains play a pivotal role in the lives of athletes, coaches, and team staff by offering guidance, encouragement, and comfort during moments of triumph and adversity. This chapter explores how chaplains, equipped with essential skills like active listening, emotional intelligence, and spiritual wisdom, provide unwavering support and foster resilience. Their ability to navigate the dual spectrums of highs and lows not only builds trust but also serves as a source of strength for those they minister to.

The Chaplain's Role in High Moments

Celebrating Success

In moments of triumph, chaplains help athletes remain grounded. Victories often bring an overwhelming rush of emotion—joy, relief, pride, and even pressure to maintain performance. A chaplain provides spiritual grounding by reminding athletes to attribute their success to hard work, teamwork, and divine blessings.

Biblical Perspective on Humility in Success

A chaplain often references verses like *Proverbs 16:18*—"Pride goes before destruction, and a haughty spirit before a fall"—to teach the importance of humility. They may lead celebratory prayers, emphasizing gratitude to God for the opportunity and achievements.

Enhancing Team Unity

Victories can sometimes create divisions within a team due to competition or individual achievements overshadowing collective goals. Chaplains act as mediators, helping team members focus on unity and shared purpose through motivational talks and team-building prayer sessions.

Example from the Field

During the 2016 Summer Olympics, several athletes from the U.S. track team credited their team chaplain with helping them stay humble and focused on their mission. By leading post-victory devotions, the chaplain encouraged them to view their wins as opportunities to inspire others and glorify God.

The Chaplain's Role in Low Moments

Offering Comfort in Defeat

Losses in sports often lead to feelings of guilt, frustration, and doubt. Chaplains provide a safe and non-judgmental space where athletes can process their emotions. Through empathetic conversations and scriptural encouragement, they help athletes find hope in adversity.

Scriptural Encouragement for Resilience

Verses like *2 Corinthians 4:8-9*—"We are hard-pressed on every side, but not crushed; perplexed, but not in despair; persecuted, but not abandoned; struck down, but not destroyed"—remind athletes that failure is temporary and part of a greater journey.

Preventing Isolation

In times of personal or professional failure, athletes may retreat into isolation. Chaplains counter this by reaching out proactively, offering companionship, and involving them in communal activities like team devotions or support groups.

Example of Redemption through Chaplaincy

A professional basketball player, battling with depression after missing the game-winning shot in a playoff match, found solace in his team chaplain. By sharing stories of biblical figures who overcame failures—such as Peter denying Jesus and later becoming a leader of the early church—the chaplain helped the player regain confidence and perspective.

Active Listening: The Cornerstone of Chaplaincy Support

The Importance of Active Listening

Active listening is a vital skill for chaplains, enabling them to deeply understand and empathize with the emotions and experiences of those they serve. By being fully present, chaplains create an environment where individuals feel heard, valued, and supported.

Key elements of active listening include:

- **Presence:** Maintaining eye contact, avoiding interruptions, and showing genuine interest.
- **Empathy:** Reflecting on the speaker's emotions and validating their experiences.
- **Clarification:** Asking open-ended questions to ensure a deeper understanding.

Fostering Trust through Listening

Athletes, often under immense pressure, need a safe outlet to express their fears and vulnerabilities. Chaplains, through active listening, build trust and create strong, supportive relationships.

Case Study

A collegiate soccer team chaplain shared how active listening helped a struggling midfielder overcome self-doubt. The chaplain's attentive presence allowed the athlete to share their concerns openly, leading to tailored spiritual guidance that ultimately restored their confidence.

Emotional Intelligence in Chaplaincy

Chaplains navigate complex emotional landscapes, requiring a high degree of emotional intelligence (EI). EI helps chaplains manage their emotions, read the feelings of others, and respond with compassion.

Developing Emotional Intelligence

- **Self-Awareness:** Recognizing their own emotional triggers to remain calm and composed.
- **Empathy:** Understanding the unspoken emotions of athletes, such as anxiety or fear.
- **Social Skills:** Building rapport and maintaining long-term relationships with teams.

Example of Emotional Intelligence in Action

During a championship loss, a chaplain demonstrated EI by identifying the team's collective despair and leading a post-game reflection. Instead of focusing on the defeat, the chaplain encouraged gratitude for the journey, fostering a sense of hope for the future.

Navigating Professional Challenges

Managing Ethical Boundaries

Chaplains often walk a fine line between being a friend and a spiritual guide. They must maintain ethical boundaries to ensure trust and respect within their relationships.

Overcoming Resistance

Not all athletes may be open to spiritual guidance. Chaplains use patience and inclusivity, ensuring their support is accessible to believers and non-believers alike.

Future Strategies

To enhance their impact, chaplains should:

1. Pursue ongoing training in emotional intelligence and counseling.
2. Develop culturally sensitive approaches to cater to diverse teams.
3. Collaborate with psychologists and coaches for holistic athlete care.

The Future of Chaplaincy in Sports

To ensure chaplaincy continues to thrive in the sports world, its role must expand beyond the traditional focus on prayer and counseling. Chaplains should be integrated into team cultures, serving as holistic support systems that address the spiritual, emotional, and professional needs of athletes.

Conclusion

Chaplains are indispensable allies in the world of sports, providing unwavering support during the highs of victory and the lows of defeat. By mastering skills like active listening and emotional intelligence, chaplains help athletes navigate the complex dynamics of competition while fostering personal growth and resilience. As sports continue to evolve, so must chaplaincy—ensuring its relevance and impact remain steadfast in an ever-changing landscape.

Spiritual Lessons Learned from Sports

Sports provide a rich environment for spiritual growth, reflection, and the application of faith principles. For chaplains, the integration of sports and spirituality creates unique opportunities to engage with athletes, coaches, and the broader sports community in meaningful ways. By examining sports through the lens of *missio Dei* (the mission of God), chaplains see their ministry as a way to reveal God's presence and love to everyone they encounter. This chapter explores the spiritual lessons learned from sports, emphasizing the transformative power of chaplaincy in athletic contexts.

1. Viewing Sports Chaplaincy through the Lens of Missio Dei

The concept of *missio Dei* highlights that God's mission is not confined to religious spaces but extends into all aspects of life, including sports. Sports chaplaincy becomes an avenue through which God's love, grace, and purpose are revealed. Chaplains who approach their ministry with this mindset see sports as a divine platform to:

- Share the Gospel with athletes, believers, and non-believers alike.
- Model Christ-like character through service and compassion.
- Encourage others to view their talents and achievements as gifts from God.

Example of Missio Dei in Action

An Australian sports chaplain shared how his consistent presence during training and matches led to deeper conversations about faith among players. By embodying humility and integrity, he became a living testimony of God's mission in their lives.

2. Education, Training, and Practice in Sports Chaplaincy

Sports chaplaincy requires a well-rounded understanding of ministry frameworks and the nuances of athletic culture. The role goes beyond traditional pastoral care by emphasizing the importance of contextualizing spiritual guidance to fit the unique needs of sports environments.

Key Elements of Chaplaincy Training

- **Educational Preparation:** Courses on theology, pastoral care, and sports psychology equip chaplains to address the physical and emotional challenges athletes face.
- **Practical Experience:** Active involvement in sports teams allows chaplains to build trust and credibility.
- **Spiritual Consistency:** Aligning chaplaincy practices with personal faith and theological themes ensures authenticity in ministry.

---

3. Spiritual Lessons from Game Day Ministry

Prayer and Divine Protection

College chaplains often pray for the safety of athletes before games. These prayers not only seek God's protection but also serve as a reminder that faith underpins all aspects of life, including competition.

The Power of Community

Standing in the press box or joining the sidelines allows chaplains to observe the dynamics of teamwork, dedication, and resilience. These moments underscore biblical principles such as unity (*Psalm 133:1*: "How good and pleasant it is when God's people live together in unity!") and perseverance (*Hebrews 12:1*: "Let us run with perseverance the race marked out for us.").

4. Integrating Theology and Sports

A critical aspect of chaplaincy is the integration of theological themes and personal beliefs into sports ministry. Chaplains must reflect on their spiritual metaphors and images to convey messages that resonate with athletes.

Key Theological Themes in Sports Chaplaincy

- **Victory and Humility:** Teaching athletes to celebrate success with gratitude while remaining humble.
- **Suffering and Resilience:** Helping athletes view challenges as opportunities for growth, akin to Christ's perseverance on the cross.
- **Purpose and Calling:** Encouraging athletes to see their talents as part of God's plan for their lives.

5. Research Insights: The Role of Christian Sports Chaplains in Australia

Research conducted on sports chaplaincy in contemporary Australia reveals the impact of Christian chaplains in shaping team cultures and individual lives. Findings highlight the chaplain's ability to:

- Foster inclusivity and respect among team members.
- Provide emotional and spiritual support during times of crisis.
- Serve as a bridge between sports organizations and faith communities.

Case Study

In one Australian football team, the chaplain's consistent support during a player's injury recovery inspired the entire team to value perseverance and faith. The chaplain's presence reinforced the importance of a holistic approach to well-being, blending physical, mental, and spiritual care.

6. Transformational Lessons for Athletes and Chaplains

For Athletes

Athletes often learn to:

- Embrace their identity beyond performance, recognizing their worth as God's creation.
- Develop a deeper sense of purpose by aligning their goals with spiritual values.

- Overcome adversity by relying on faith as a source of strength and guidance.

For Chaplains

Chaplains gain insights into the importance of adaptability, patience, and cultural sensitivity in ministry. They also witness firsthand the transformative power of faith in helping individuals navigate success and failure.

---

7. Challenges and Opportunities

While the integration of spirituality in sports brings numerous benefits, chaplains must navigate challenges such as:

- Addressing the diverse beliefs of team members while maintaining inclusivity.
- Balancing the demands of competitive sports with the need for spiritual reflection.
- Ensuring that chaplaincy remains relevant and impactful in rapidly evolving sports cultures.

Future Directions

To maximize their impact, chaplains should:

1. Engage in continuous professional development to stay informed about best practices in ministry and sports psychology.
2. Collaborate with coaches, psychologists, and other support staff to provide holistic care.

3. Advocate for the inclusion of chaplaincy in all levels of sports, from amateur leagues to professional organizations.

Conclusion

Sports chaplaincy offers profound opportunities to learn and teach spiritual lessons. By viewing their ministry through the lens of *missio Dei*, chaplains bring God's presence into the dynamic and competitive world of sports. Through education, practice, and a commitment to integrating theology with athletics, chaplains empower athletes to grow in faith, character, and purpose. As research and practical experiences continue to shed light on the transformative potential of chaplaincy, it becomes clear that its lessons extend far beyond the playing field, touching the hearts and souls of all who participate.

CHAPTER 06

BEYOND THE GAME-LIFE AFTER SPORTS

Athletes dedicate much of their lives to pursuing excellence in their chosen sport. However, the conclusion of an athletic career often marks the beginning of a challenging transition period. Life after sports presents unique emotional, mental, and social challenges, requiring athletes to navigate a new sense of purpose and identity. Sports chaplaincy plays a crucial role in addressing these challenges by providing holistic support that encompasses the emotional, spiritual, and practical aspects of life beyond the game. This chapter explores how chaplaincy aids athletes in building a fulfilling post-sports life while maintaining their value orientation and mental well-being.

1. Challenges of Life After Sports

The transition from competitive sports to life beyond the game is often accompanied by significant challenges:

- **Sense of Loss**: Athletes frequently experience a profound sense of loss as they step away from the structured environment of sports. The absence of competition, camaraderie, and routine can lead to feelings of emptiness.
- **Identity Crisis**: For many athletes, their identity is deeply intertwined with their athletic achievements. Retirement often brings the question: "Who am I without my sport?"
- **Mental Health Struggles**: The pressures of redefining one's purpose, coupled with the loss of recognition and routine, can lead to anxiety, depression, or other mental health issues.
- **Navigating Relationships**: Athletes often face difficulties in maintaining or redefining relationships as their focus shifts from sports to personal and familial life.
- **Career Transition**: Many athletes struggle to translate the skills they've honed on the field into a new professional setting.

---

2. The Role of Chaplaincy in Supporting Life After Sports

Sports chaplaincy offers a comprehensive support system to help athletes address these challenges effectively. Chaplains provide personalized care, focusing on the person behind the athlete and fostering their holistic development.

Emotional and Spiritual Support

- **Active Listening**: Chaplains create a safe and non-judgmental space for athletes to express their struggles, helping them process emotions tied to retirement and change.

- **Guidance and Reflection**: By encouraging self-reflection, chaplains help athletes explore their identity beyond sports, emphasizing their intrinsic worth as individuals created in the image of God.
- **Spiritual Strengthening**: Chaplains guide athletes to rely on their faith for strength and clarity during this transitional phase. Biblical teachings such as *Jeremiah 29:11* ("For I know the plans I have for you") provide hope and assurance of a purposeful future.

Practical Transition Assistance

- **Work-Life Balance**: Chaplains help athletes establish healthy routines that integrate family, work, and self-care, fostering a sense of stability.
- **Career Mentorship**: Chaplains connect athletes with resources to explore new career paths, leveraging their discipline, teamwork, and leadership skills.

Community Building

- Chaplains encourage athletes to stay connected to a supportive community, reducing feelings of isolation. They may facilitate small groups, mentorship programs, or community engagement opportunities that allow retired athletes to maintain a sense of purpose.

3. Programs and Initiatives: Beyond Gold

The "Beyond Gold" initiative exemplifies how sports chaplaincy can holistically support athletes throughout and beyond their careers.

Key Principles of Beyond Gold

1. **Respect for Diversity**: Beyond Gold respects every athlete's religious and cultural background, creating a trustful and inclusive environment.
2. **Value Orientation**: The initiative focuses on guiding athletes to uphold values such as integrity, resilience, and service to others.
3. **Mental Strength Development**: Chaplains help athletes build mental resilience through counseling, mindfulness practices, and spiritual disciplines.

Stages of Support

1. **Active Career Phase**: Supporting athletes in managing pressures, maintaining balance, and planning for life beyond sports.
2. **Transition Phase**: Providing emotional, spiritual, and practical guidance during the shift from active sports to retirement.
3. **Post-Retirement Phase**: Empowering athletes to redefine their purpose, develop new skills, and inspire others as role models.

---

4. Case Studies: Transformative Impact

Case Study 1: Rebuilding Identity

An elite swimmer struggled with depression after retiring from a 10-year career. A chaplain helped her rediscover her sense of purpose by encouraging her to mentor younger swimmers and pursue a teaching career. Today, she credits her chaplain's guidance for her newfound joy and fulfillment.

Case Study 2: Career Transition

A retired football player partnered with his chaplain to develop a plan for starting a fitness training business. With the chaplain's mentorship and network connections, he successfully transitioned into entrepreneurship, becoming a community leader.

---

5. Spiritual Lessons in Life After Sports

The lessons learned through sports chaplaincy extend far beyond athletic performance. Athletes are reminded that their worth is not tied to medals or records but to their identity as beloved children of God. Biblical principles such as resilience (*Philippians 4:13*: "I can do all things through Christ") and service (*Matthew 23:11*: "The greatest among you will be your servant") guide athletes in leading impactful lives post-retirement.

---

6. Future Directions for Chaplaincy

As sports chaplaincy continues to evolve, the following steps can enhance its impact:

1. **Increased Awareness**: Promoting the benefits of chaplaincy to sports organizations, schools, and communities.
2. **Specialized Training**: Developing programs focused on post-retirement care for chaplains.
3. **Collaborative Networks**: Partnering with psychologists, career counselors, and community organizations to provide comprehensive support.
4. **Research and Advocacy**: Conducting studies on the long-term benefits of chaplaincy for athletes and advocating for its inclusion in sports programs worldwide.

7. Conclusion

Life after sports presents a pivotal moment of transformation for athletes. Sports chaplaincy, through its holistic and compassionate approach, empowers athletes to navigate this transition with grace and resilience. By addressing emotional, spiritual, and practical needs, chaplains help athletes redefine their identity, embrace their new phase of life, and continue to inspire as role models in society. Initiatives like Beyond Gold exemplify the potential of chaplaincy to make a lasting difference, reinforcing the message that an athlete's value extends far beyond their achievements on the field. Together, chaplaincy and sports can weave a tapestry of purpose, faith, and humanity that inspires generations to come.

Transitioning from Active Sports to Life Beyond the Field

The transition from active sports to life beyond the field is one of the most challenging periods in an athlete's life. For many, the conclusion of a sports career brings uncertainty, loss of identity, and a search for new purpose. Chaplaincy provides a critical support framework during this transition, offering spiritual, emotional, and practical guidance. This chapter examines how chaplaincy facilitates this shift, the common challenges athletes face, and how tailored chaplaincy strategies can help ensure a smooth and meaningful transition.

1. Challenges Faced by Athletes During Transition

Athletes often struggle with the following challenges as they move from competitive sports to life beyond the field:

- **Loss of Identity**: Athletes commonly associate their self-worth with their performance and achievements. The end of their sports career can lead to an identity crisis.
- **Sense of Loss and Grief**: Retiring from sports can feel like a loss of purpose, routine, and community, similar to grieving a significant loss.
- **Mental Health Issues**: Anxiety, depression, and feelings of isolation are prevalent among retired athletes who struggle to redefine their place in society.
- **Career Uncertainty**: Transitioning to a new career is daunting, especially when skills honed in sports don't seem to translate directly into other professional fields.
- **Financial Instability**: For some athletes, the end of their sports career may mean the end of their primary source of income, leading to financial stress.

2. The Role of Chaplaincy in Transition

Chaplains are uniquely positioned to help athletes navigate the transition from active sports to life beyond the field by addressing their holistic needs: spiritual, emotional, and practical.

2.1 Spiritual Support

- **Redefining Identity in Faith**: Chaplains guide athletes to find their identity in their spiritual beliefs rather than in their athletic achievements. Passages such as *Psalm 139:14* ("I am fearfully and wonderfully made") help athletes understand their intrinsic worth beyond their profession.
- **Purpose in God's Plan**: By emphasizing that each individual has a role in God's plan (*Jeremiah 29:11*: "For I know the plans I have for you"), chaplains help athletes embrace a hopeful future.

2.2 Emotional Guidance

- **Active Listening**: Chaplains provide a safe space for athletes to express their feelings, fears, and uncertainties. This empathetic support helps athletes process their emotions constructively.
- **Encouragement and Motivation**: Chaplains act as encouragers, reminding athletes of their resilience and ability to overcome challenges.

2.3 Practical Assistance

- **Career Counseling and Networking**: Chaplains often collaborate with career counselors to help athletes explore new professional opportunities and develop transferable skills such as leadership and teamwork.
- **Financial Guidance**: Chaplains connect athletes with financial advisors who can assist with budgeting, investments, and long-term financial planning.

---

3. Strategies for Effective Chaplaincy in Transition

To effectively support athletes during this period, chaplains employ the following strategies:

3.1 Mentorship and Role Modeling

Chaplains connect retiring athletes with mentors who have successfully navigated similar transitions. This guidance provides practical advice and emotional reassurance.

3.2 Community Building

Through small groups, workshops, and faith-based gatherings, chaplains help athletes build new communities, reducing feelings of isolation.

3.3 Holistic Development Programs

Programs like Beyond Gold focus on physical, mental, and spiritual well-being, providing athletes with a comprehensive framework to address all aspects of their transition.

4. Case Studies of Chaplaincy Impact

Case Study 1: Spiritual Renewal

A professional basketball player struggled with depression after retiring from a 15-year career. A chaplain helped him rediscover his faith and channel his energy into community service. Through volunteering and mentoring youth, he found renewed purpose and fulfillment.

Case Study 2: Career Transition

A former soccer player faced difficulty transitioning into the corporate world. With the chaplain's support, he identified leadership skills developed on the field and successfully applied them in a managerial role.

Case Study 3: Overcoming Isolation

A retired swimmer felt isolated after leaving the structured environment of sports. A chaplain introduced her to a faith-based peer support group where she connected with others experiencing similar transitions, leading to meaningful friendships and spiritual growth.

5. Future Directions for Chaplaincy in Transition Support

To expand the impact of chaplaincy in transition, the following steps are recommended:

- **Developing Specialized Training**: Chaplains should receive training in post-career counseling, financial literacy, and mental health support tailored to athletes.
- **Creating Structured Programs**: Sports organizations should partner with chaplains to create formal programs addressing retirement preparation, including workshops on career planning, mental health, and spirituality.
- **Collaborating with Stakeholders**: Chaplains can collaborate with coaches, sports psychologists, and community leaders to provide a multi-disciplinary approach to transition support.
- **Promoting Research and Awareness**: Continued research into the role of chaplaincy in athlete transitions will help refine strategies and promote its value to sports organizations and society at large.

---

6. Spiritual Lessons in Transition

Chaplains emphasize the spiritual lessons learned during the transition:

- **Resilience Through Faith**: Transitions, though challenging, strengthen character and faith.
- **Purpose Beyond Performance**: True fulfillment comes from living a purpose-driven life, not just achieving accolades.

- **Service to Others**: Retired athletes can use their platform and experiences to inspire and mentor future generations.

7. Conclusion

The transition from active sports to life beyond the field is a complex and multifaceted process that requires holistic support. Chaplaincy serves as a vital resource, guiding athletes through the emotional, spiritual, and practical challenges of this significant life change. By fostering resilience, building new communities, and offering spiritual grounding, chaplains help athletes not only transition successfully but also thrive in their post-sports lives.

Through intentional strategies and collaborative efforts, chaplaincy can continue to play a transformative role, reminding athletes that their worth and purpose extend far beyond the game.

Chaplain's Support in Career Changes and Personal Growth

Athletes face significant challenges when transitioning from a career in competitive sports to life beyond the field. This period often involves redefining personal identity, exploring new career opportunities, and addressing emotional and psychological concerns. Chaplains play a crucial role in facilitating this transition, providing holistic support that fosters career growth and personal development. This chapter explores the multifaceted role of chaplains in helping athletes navigate career changes and achieve personal growth.

1. Challenges of Career Changes for Athletes

1.1 Identity Crisis

Athletes often derive their sense of self from their sports career. Transitioning away from competitive sports can lead to:

- **Loss of Purpose**: Without the structure and goals of their sports career, athletes may feel adrift.
- **Self-Worth Issues**: Performance-driven environments can condition athletes to equate their value with achievements.

1.2 Emotional and Psychological Challenges

- **Stress and Anxiety**: Uncertainty about future careers can lead to heightened stress levels.
- **Mental Health Struggles**: Depression and feelings of isolation are common during this transitional period.

1.3 Practical Challenges

- **Skill Translation**: Athletes may struggle to see how their sports-specific skills translate to other industries.
- **Networking and Opportunities**: Limited exposure to non-sports career opportunities can hinder their progress.

2. The Chaplain's Role in Supporting Career Changes

2.1 Spiritual Guidance

- **Redefining Purpose**: Chaplains help athletes understand that their value transcends their career. Biblical teachings, such as *Jeremiah 29:11* ("For I know the plans I have for you"), reassure athletes of a meaningful future.
- **Faith in Transitions**: Encouraging athletes to trust in divine guidance provides comfort and hope during uncertain times.

2.2 Emotional Support

- **Active Listening**: Chaplains offer a safe and nonjudgmental space for athletes to express fears, frustrations, and aspirations.
- **Empathy and Encouragement**: By walking alongside athletes, chaplains provide reassurance that they are not alone in their journey.

2.3 Practical Assistance

- **Career Exploration**: Chaplains assist athletes in identifying interests and strengths that align with potential career paths.
- **Skill Development**: They encourage athletes to develop transferable skills such as leadership, teamwork, and discipline cultivated during their sports careers.

3. Chaplains as Facilitators of Personal Growth

3.1 Building Resilience

- **Lessons from Sports**: Athletes often develop perseverance, adaptability, and focus through their sports careers. Chaplains help them apply these qualities to personal and professional challenges.
- **Spiritual Resilience**: By fostering a strong spiritual foundation, chaplains help athletes navigate life's uncertainties with faith and strength.

3.2 Encouraging Lifelong Learning

- Chaplains motivate athletes to pursue education, training, or certifications that open new career opportunities.
- They promote a mindset of continuous growth, emphasizing that learning does not stop with the end of a sports career.

3.3 Enhancing Relationships

- **Rebuilding Connections**: Retirement from sports often disrupts social circles. Chaplains encourage athletes to rebuild and strengthen personal and professional networks.
- **Family Support**: Chaplains provide guidance on navigating family dynamics during transitional periods.

4. Case Studies and Evidence

Case Study 1: From Player to Mentor

A retired professional soccer player struggled with feelings of insignificance after leaving the game. Through chaplaincy, he discovered a passion for coaching and mentoring youth. The chaplain guided him to align his skills with his desire to impact the next generation, leading to a fulfilling career as a youth coach.

Case Study 2: Overcoming Financial Uncertainty

A track and field athlete faced financial challenges after retirement. With the chaplain's support, the athlete pursued further education and secured a position in sports management, achieving stability and a sense of purpose.

Case Study 3: Personal Transformation Through Faith

A retired basketball player turned to faith-based community service after working with a chaplain. The player found renewed purpose in helping underserved communities, inspired by the spiritual lessons shared by the chaplain.

---

5. Strategies for Effective Chaplaincy Support

5.1 Holistic Counseling

- Chaplains integrate spiritual, emotional, and practical guidance to provide comprehensive support tailored to each athlete's needs.

5.2 Career Transition Programs

- Collaboration with career coaches and mentors ensures athletes have access to resources and opportunities that facilitate career growth.

5.3 Focus on Spiritual Growth

- Chaplains emphasize the importance of spiritual growth as a foundation for personal and professional success.

6. The Future of Chaplaincy in Career Changes

To enhance their impact, chaplains can:

- **Expand Educational Opportunities**: Partnering with universities and training programs to offer scholarships and courses for athletes.
- **Foster Mentorship Networks**: Connecting retired athletes with professionals in various fields to provide guidance and encouragement.
- **Advocate for Chaplaincy in Sports Organizations**: Raising awareness about the benefits of chaplaincy in supporting athletes through life transitions.

7. Conclusion

Chaplains play a pivotal role in helping athletes navigate career changes and achieve personal growth. By addressing spiritual, emotional, and practical challenges, chaplains empower athletes to find new purpose and direction in life. Through holistic counseling and unwavering support, chaplains ensure that athletes' transitions are not only smooth but transformative, enabling them to lead fulfilling and impactful lives beyond their sports careers.

The role of chaplaincy in this area extends beyond individual athletes, fostering a broader culture of resilience, growth, and faith within the sports community. With strategic efforts and collaboration, chaplains can continue to inspire and uplift athletes as they embrace life's next chapter.

Maintaining Faith and Purpose After Sports

Transitioning from the structured, high-pressure world of sports to life beyond competition often presents athletes with significant challenges. Many athletes struggle to maintain the sense of faith and purpose they once found on the field. Chaplains, as spiritual guides and mentors, play an essential role in helping athletes navigate this shift, ensuring that their faith remains a cornerstone of their identity and that they find renewed purpose in life after sports.

1. The Importance of Faith and Purpose Post-Sports

For many athletes, faith and purpose have been intricately tied to their sports careers. The discipline, teamwork, and goals inherent in athletic competition often mirror spiritual principles, giving athletes a clear sense of direction. However, retirement can disrupt this equilibrium, leading to:

- **Identity Crises**: Without the platform of competition, athletes may struggle to define who they are.
- **Loss of Routine**: Sports often provide a daily structure that gives life meaning.
- **Emotional and Spiritual Void**: Many athletes find themselves disconnected from the faith practices that once sustained them.

---

2. Chaplains as Navigators of Faith and Purpose

Chaplains provide critical support during this transitional phase, helping athletes reconnect with their faith and discover new avenues for purpose.

2.1 Reaffirming Spiritual Identity

- **Personalized Devotions**: Chaplains create tailored devotional practices that resonate with the athlete's post-sports life.
- **Scriptural Guidance**: Biblical teachings, such as *Philippians 3:13-14* ("Forgetting what is behind and straining toward what is ahead"), offer encouragement and direction.

- **Faith Community Engagement**: Chaplains connect athletes with faith-based communities where they can continue to grow spiritually.

2.2 Helping Athletes Redefine Purpose

- **Exploring God's Calling**: Chaplains guide athletes in seeking divine purpose beyond sports, whether through service, mentorship, or new careers.
- **Goal Setting**: Helping athletes establish meaningful goals that align with their values and faith.
- **Purpose-Driven Activities**: Encouraging involvement in activities like community outreach or coaching, which provide a renewed sense of significance.

---

3. Practical Strategies Chaplains Employ

3.1 Providing Ongoing Spiritual Counseling

- **Addressing Emotional Needs**: Chaplains offer support to help athletes cope with feelings of loss or disconnection.
- **Developing Resilience**: Using faith-based practices, such as prayer and meditation, to build spiritual strength.

3.2 Offering Faith-Based Career Transition Programs

- **Skill Identification**: Assisting athletes in identifying their God-given talents and how they can apply them in new contexts.

- **Mentorship Networks**: Introducing athletes to mentors who share similar faith-based values and have successfully transitioned to new careers.

3.3 Establishing Faith-Centered Rituals

- **Daily Devotions**: Encouraging athletes to maintain regular Bible reading and prayer.
- **Spiritual Retreats**: Organizing retreats where athletes can reflect, renew their faith, and connect with others in similar situations.

3.4 Community Building

- **Creating Support Groups**: Forming peer groups of retired athletes to share experiences and support one another.
- **Faith Integration Events**: Hosting workshops and seminars that integrate faith with practical skills like financial planning or personal development.

4. Success Stories: Maintaining Faith and Purpose

4.1 From Champion to Mentor

A retired Olympic swimmer struggled with depression after retirement. With the chaplain's support, she found purpose in mentoring young athletes, teaching them how faith shaped her journey. This role allowed her to find joy and purpose in serving others.

4.2 Overcoming Financial and Spiritual Challenges

A professional football player, burdened with financial difficulties and spiritual disconnection, sought help from a chaplain. Through counseling, the chaplain guided him to pursue a career in sports ministry, blending his passion for faith and athletics.

4.3 Building a Legacy Beyond Sports

A basketball player turned to chaplaincy himself, inspired by the guidance he received during his transition. His faith journey not only transformed his life but also allowed him to inspire others facing similar struggles.

---

5. Challenges Chaplains Face and How to Address Them

5.1 Resistance to Spiritual Practices

Not all athletes are ready to embrace faith or rediscover it after sports. Chaplains must adopt a patient and empathetic approach, focusing on relationship-building.

5.2 Lack of Institutional Support

Chaplains sometimes struggle to gain access to resources or institutional backing for post-sports ministry. Advocacy and partnerships with faith organizations can help overcome these hurdles.

5.3 Balancing Spiritual and Practical Needs

Athletes often face immediate practical concerns, such as employment or financial stability. Chaplains must collaborate with career counselors and other professionals to offer holistic support.

6. The Future of Chaplaincy in Post-Sports Life

6.1 Expanding Chaplaincy Training

Training chaplains to address the specific needs of retired athletes ensures they are equipped to provide effective support.

6.2 Promoting Awareness of Chaplaincy

Sports organizations and faith communities should recognize the value of chaplaincy in post-sports transitions, advocating for its inclusion in retirement planning.

6.3 Building Collaborative Networks

Partnering with career development programs, mental health professionals, and community organizations enhances the chaplain's ability to meet diverse needs.

7. Conclusion

Maintaining faith and purpose after sports is a vital aspect of an athlete's transition to life beyond the field. Chaplains play a transformative role in this process, guiding athletes to reconnect with their spiritual identity and find new purpose in their post-sports journey.

By offering personalized spiritual guidance, fostering community, and addressing practical challenges, chaplains help athletes navigate this often-difficult phase with faith and hope. Through their efforts, athletes can lead fulfilling lives that honor their God-given talents and inspire those around them. As the importance of chaplaincy grows, its integration into post-sports planning will undoubtedly become a cornerstone of holistic athlete care.

CHAPTER 07

COMMUNITY AND SERVICE

Chaplains in the Community

Chaplains play a vital role in fostering unity, offering guidance, and serving as beacons of hope in their communities. Their presence extends beyond their traditional roles within institutions such as sports teams, hospitals, or the military. By embedding themselves in the broader fabric of society, chaplains address spiritual, emotional, and practical needs, often bridging gaps where other support systems fail.

1. The Importance of Chaplains in the Community

Communities thrive when individuals have access to holistic care—support that addresses the mind, body, and spirit. Chaplains contribute to this by:

1.1 Addressing Spiritual Needs

- Many individuals and families face spiritual crises that leave them feeling disconnected or lost. Chaplains provide a non-judgmental ear and guidance rooted in faith and compassion.
- Evidence: A study conducted by the Journal of Pastoral Care highlights how chaplains in urban communities reduce feelings of isolation among marginalized populations by facilitating faith-based programs.

1.2 Promoting Mental and Emotional Wellness

- Chaplains offer counseling to individuals grappling with grief, anxiety, depression, or other emotional challenges. Their faith-informed perspective helps individuals find meaning and resilience in difficult times.

1.3 Building Social Cohesion

- Through community events, prayer gatherings, and interfaith dialogues, chaplains foster unity across diverse groups. They serve as neutral figures who encourage understanding and collaboration.

1.4 Providing Crisis Response

- In times of disaster, tragedy, or communal unrest, chaplains are often the first responders, offering spiritual and emotional care to those affected.

2. Services Chaplains Should Offer in the Community

To address the needs of a dynamic and diverse community, chaplains should provide a range of services that reflect compassion, inclusivity, and practical support.

2.1 Spiritual Guidance and Worship

- **Regular Services**: Chaplains can organize prayer meetings, Bible studies, and worship services open to all members of the community.
- **Personalized Counseling**: Offering one-on-one spiritual counseling tailored to individuals' unique struggles and goals.

2.2 Grief and Trauma Support

- Providing support for families dealing with loss or tragedy, such as organizing memorial services and grief counseling sessions.
- Evidence: A 2022 survey by the Chaplaincy Institute found that 85% of individuals who received grief counseling from chaplains reported feeling more at peace and supported in their recovery.

2.3 Educational Programs

- **Workshops on Faith and Resilience**: Teaching community members how to draw strength from their faith during times of difficulty.

- **Youth Mentorship**: Leading programs that inspire young people to adopt positive values, avoid destructive behaviors, and develop a sense of purpose.

2.4 Community Outreach and Advocacy

- **Feeding Programs**: Partnering with local organizations to distribute food and other resources to the needy.
- **Advocacy for Justice**: Acting as mediators and advocates for marginalized groups, ensuring that their voices are heard in civic discussions.

2.5 Crisis Intervention

- **Disaster Response**: Assisting communities affected by natural disasters through prayer, comfort, and logistical support.
- **Conflict Mediation**: Helping resolve disputes within families or neighborhoods through faith-based counseling.

3. The Transformative Impact of Chaplaincy in Communities

3.1 Fostering Hope in Difficult Times

- Example: Following a natural disaster in Louisiana, chaplains from a local church organized relief camps, offering both material aid and spiritual solace. Their efforts not only provided immediate relief but also encouraged community members to rebuild with a sense of hope and resilience.

3.2 Building Inclusive Spaces

- Chaplains often create spaces where individuals of different faiths, ethnicities, and backgrounds can come together for mutual understanding. This inclusivity fosters a sense of belonging and reduces social tensions.
- Evidence: Research from the Harvard Divinity School indicates that interfaith chaplaincy programs significantly reduce incidents of hate crime in diverse communities.

3.3 Inspiring Volunteerism and Service

- By modeling selfless service, chaplains inspire others to get involved in community-building activities, creating a ripple effect of compassion and generosity.

---

4. Challenges and How Chaplains Overcome Them

4.1 Resistance to Religious Involvement

- Some individuals may mistrust or reject faith-based services, viewing them as irrelevant or intrusive. Chaplains must adopt an open-minded and inclusive approach, respecting diverse beliefs while offering support.

4.2 Resource Limitations

- Many chaplains operate on limited budgets, which can restrict the scope of their work. Partnering with community organizations and leveraging volunteer networks can help overcome this hurdle.

4.3 Balancing Spiritual and Practical Needs

- Communities often have immediate needs, such as food or housing, that take precedence over spiritual care. Chaplains must integrate practical support with their spiritual mission to address the whole person.

5. The Future of Community Chaplaincy

As communities evolve, so must chaplaincy. Future efforts should focus on:

- **Enhanced Training**: Equipping chaplains with skills in trauma counseling, interfaith dialogue, and community organizing.
- **Technology Integration**: Using social media and online platforms to reach and engage more people.
- **Expanding Roles**: Including chaplaincy in sectors like education, local governance, and social justice advocacy to maximize its impact.

6. Conclusion

Chaplains are indispensable to the health and vitality of communities. Through their commitment to spiritual guidance, emotional support, and practical service, they address the holistic needs of individuals and groups. Whether through grief counseling, youth mentorship, or disaster response, chaplains offer hope, unity, and purpose to those they serve.

In an increasingly complex and fractured world, the presence of chaplains in our communities stands as a testament to the power of compassion and faith. Their work reminds us that, regardless of our circumstances, we are all connected by a shared humanity that thrives on understanding, service, and love. By supporting and expanding community chaplaincy efforts, we can create stronger, more harmonious societies for generations to come.

Outreach and Community Service Initiatives Led by Chaplains

Chaplains, through their ministry of presence, significantly impact the communities they serve. By embedding themselves in businesses, schools, shelters, and other community settings, they build supportive relationships and foster environments of trust, care, and encouragement. These outreach and service initiatives not only meet immediate needs but also create opportunities for holistic transformation in individuals and communities.

---

1. The Ministry of Presence

The concept of the "ministry of presence" is foundational to chaplaincy. It involves being physically present, emotionally available, and spiritually attuned to the needs of individuals and groups.

1.1 The Role of Presence

- Chaplains offer comfort through active listening, empathy, and spiritual guidance. Their presence conveys care, even in the absence of immediate solutions to problems.
- In schools, chaplains mentor students, providing guidance during formative years.
- In shelters, they bring hope to displaced or distressed individuals by addressing both spiritual and material needs.

1.2 Biblical and Theological Basis

- Chaplaincy's ministry of presence aligns with the biblical mandate to "bear one another's burdens" (Galatians 6:2). It reflects the incarnational model of Christ, who lived among those He came to serve (John 1:14).

---

2. Community Chaplaincy Initiatives

Community chaplaincy provides unique opportunities to address the multifaceted needs of individuals across various settings.

2.1 Supporting Businesses

- Chaplains in workplaces contribute to employee well-being by providing counseling on stress management, conflict resolution, and work-life balance.

- Example: A chaplain embedded in a manufacturing company reported reduced employee turnover and increased morale after implementing weekly wellness meetings.

2.2 Addressing School Needs

- Chaplains in schools offer spiritual and emotional care to students, staff, and families. They help navigate challenges such as bullying, academic stress, and family issues.
- Example: In a qualitative study conducted in rural high schools, students reported increased self-confidence and resilience after participating in chaplain-led mentorship programs.

2.3 Serving Shelters for the Displaced and Distressed

- Chaplains work in homeless shelters, providing practical support such as food and clothing while addressing spiritual needs through prayer, Bible studies, and counseling.
- Evidence: Reports from a community chaplaincy initiative in New York revealed that 70% of shelter residents who participated in chaplain-led programs experienced improved mental health outcomes.

2.4 Engagement in the Marketplace

- Market chaplaincy involves chaplains engaging with small businesses and community hubs, offering prayer, encouragement, and mediation services.
- Example: In Kenya, market chaplains helped resolve conflicts among vendors, leading to improved cooperation and increased sales.

3. Integration of Chaplains in Community Health Initiatives

Chaplains play a pivotal role in community health initiatives, addressing not only physical health but also emotional and spiritual well-being.

3.1 Holistic Health Programs

- Community chaplains collaborate with healthcare providers to offer holistic care. This includes counseling for patients, spiritual support for families, and stress-relief workshops.
- Evidence: A qualitative study in Australia showed that chaplaincy integration in healthcare reduced hospital readmissions by 15% by promoting emotional and spiritual wellness.

3.2 Mental Health Support

- Chaplains address mental health issues, such as anxiety, depression, and trauma, particularly among vulnerable populations.
- Example: In a post-disaster setting, chaplains facilitated group therapy sessions for survivors, significantly improving their coping mechanisms.

3.3 Advocacy for Health Equity

- Chaplains advocate for underserved populations by connecting them with health resources and services.

4. Challenges Faced by Community Chaplains

While chaplaincy initiatives yield significant benefits, they also encounter several challenges:

4.1 Limited Resources

- Chaplains often operate on constrained budgets, limiting the scale of their programs.
- Solution: Partnering with local churches, NGOs, and government agencies can expand their resource base.

4.2 Resistance from Secular Communities

- Some secular communities may view chaplaincy as overly religious or unnecessary.
- Solution: Emphasizing inclusivity and offering practical, non-religious services alongside spiritual care can build trust and acceptance.

4.3 Balancing Diverse Needs

- Communities often present diverse and sometimes conflicting needs. Chaplains must navigate these dynamics sensitively.
- Solution: Training in cultural competence and conflict resolution can enhance their effectiveness.

---

5. Future Directions for Chaplaincy in Community Service

To maximize their impact, chaplaincy initiatives should:

5.1 Expand Training and Certification

- Offer specialized training in areas such as mental health first aid, trauma care, and interfaith dialogue.

5.2 Utilize Technology

- Leverage digital platforms to reach wider audiences through virtual counseling, online prayer meetings, and community forums.

5.3 Strengthen Collaboration

- Partner with educational institutions, healthcare providers, and civic organizations to create comprehensive service networks.

---

6. Conclusion

Chaplains, through their ministry of presence and community-focused initiatives, play an invaluable role in fostering holistic well-being. Their integration into businesses, schools, shelters, and healthcare systems addresses spiritual, emotional, and practical needs, creating transformative impacts. By addressing challenges and embracing innovative strategies, chaplains can continue to serve as pillars of support, bringing hope and healing to their communities.

Their work exemplifies the enduring relevance of faith-based care in contemporary society, reminding us that genuine transformation begins with empathy, service, and a commitment to the shared humanity of all.

Impact on Local Communities and Beyond

Chaplains, as spiritual care providers, play an essential role in supporting individuals and communities across diverse settings, including hospitals, prisons, schools, workplaces, and even disaster response environments. Their unique position allows them to serve as both spiritual guides and practical support systems, often reaching individuals disconnected from traditional religious or community networks. While their impact has historically been under-documented, recent qualitative and anecdotal evidence highlights the significant contributions chaplains make to the health, well-being, and resilience of communities.

1. The Role of Chaplains in Local Communities

Chaplains address various needs within their communities, from providing emotional and spiritual support to acting as advocates and mediators in crises. Their work spans beyond the confines of traditional institutions, extending into community outreach, counseling, and collaborative health and social initiatives.

1.1 Supporting Vulnerable Populations

- **Hospitals**: Chaplains provide care to patients and families during medical crises, offering comfort, guidance, and prayer. They often bridge gaps between medical care and spiritual or emotional needs.
- **Prisons**: Incarcerated individuals rely on chaplains for moral and spiritual guidance, which can lead to personal transformation and reduced recidivism.
- **Educational Institutions**: Chaplains in schools and universities help students navigate academic pressures, identity issues, and personal challenges, fostering a sense of belonging.

1.2 Community Advocacy

- Chaplains often serve as advocates for underserved populations, ensuring access to resources like healthcare, housing, and counseling services.
- Example: During the COVID-19 pandemic, chaplains organized food distribution programs for economically disadvantaged families in rural areas.

---

2. Evidence of Chaplaincy's Impact

Although systematic data on chaplaincy's impact remains limited, qualitative research and community testimonials provide compelling evidence of their value.

2.1 Mental and Emotional Well-being

- A study in healthcare chaplaincy found that patients who engaged with chaplains reported reduced anxiety and improved coping mechanisms during hospital stays.

- In prisons, chaplains' spiritual counseling has been linked to reduced behavioral incidents and higher rates of personal rehabilitation.

2.2 Community Health Outcomes

- Chaplains involved in public health campaigns often contribute to increased awareness and participation in health screenings, vaccinations, and mental health services.
- Example: In a collaborative program between chaplains and public health officials in Chicago, chaplain-led wellness workshops improved community health literacy, leading to a 20% increase in preventative care utilization.

2.3 Interfaith and Cross-Cultural Impact

- Chaplains often serve diverse populations, promoting interfaith understanding and reducing cultural tensions. Their neutral role allows them to mediate conflicts effectively.
- Evidence: In a refugee settlement in Jordan, chaplains worked with NGOs to foster peace and resilience among residents of different religious and cultural backgrounds.

---

3. Expanding Chaplaincy Beyond Institutional Walls

3.1 Integrating into Community Health

Chaplains increasingly contribute to community health initiatives by addressing social determinants of health, such as housing, education, and food security.

- **Case Study**: In South Africa, chaplains partnered with local clinics to provide spiritual and mental health support to HIV patients, leading to better treatment adherence rates.

3.2 Supporting Disaster Relief Efforts

Chaplains play a critical role in disaster response, offering psychological first aid, coordinating relief efforts, and fostering community resilience.

- Example: After Hurricane Katrina, chaplains organized grief counseling sessions and community rebuilding projects, helping residents regain stability.

3.3 Building Sustainable Relationships

Chaplains build trust within communities by consistently showing up in times of need. Their work fosters long-term relationships that serve as a foundation for ongoing community support initiatives.

4. Challenges to Measuring Chaplaincy's Impact

Despite their contributions, measuring the full impact of chaplaincy poses several challenges:

- **Lack of Standard Metrics**: Spiritual and emotional outcomes are difficult to quantify, making it hard to measure success.
- **Resource Constraints**: Many chaplaincy programs operate on limited budgets, restricting their capacity to document and evaluate their work.
- **Low Public Awareness**: Many people are unaware of the broad scope of chaplaincy services, limiting support and recognition.

5. Recommendations for Enhancing Impact

5.1 Improved Training and Certification

Chaplains should receive training in areas like mental health counseling, trauma care, and interfaith dialogue to better serve diverse populations.

5.2 Strategic Partnerships

Collaborating with local governments, NGOs, and community organizations can amplify the reach and resources of chaplaincy programs.

5.3 Data Collection and Research

Establishing robust frameworks for documenting outcomes and conducting research will provide evidence of chaplaincy's impact and guide future initiatives.

5.4 Public Education Campaigns

Raising awareness about chaplaincy's role and contributions can garner greater support and funding for their initiatives.

---

6. The Global Reach of Chaplaincy

While chaplaincy's roots are often local, its impact extends globally through shared best practices and international collaborations. Programs such as military chaplaincy, interfaith peacebuilding, and disaster response initiatives demonstrate the universal relevance of chaplaincy.

- Example: The International Federation of Chaplains and Humanitarian Services has trained chaplains in over 50 countries, addressing needs in healthcare, education, and social services.

---

7. Conclusion

Chaplains are indispensable to the health and vitality of local communities and beyond. Through their ministry of presence, they meet immediate spiritual and emotional needs while fostering long-term resilience and transformation. Whether in hospitals, schools, prisons, or community outreach initiatives, chaplains provide hope and guidance where it is needed most.

Expanding support for chaplaincy programs, improving their integration into broader social systems, and documenting their impact more effectively will ensure that their contributions continue to enrich communities worldwide. Chaplaincy remains a powerful testament to the enduring relevance of compassionate care in an increasingly complex and interconnected world.

Stories of Athletes Giving Back

Athletes often rise to prominence through hard work, talent, and determination. Many also carry a sense of gratitude for the communities, teams, and individuals who supported them along the way. Inspired by chaplaincy, their faith, or a desire to make a difference, numerous athletes use their platform to give back in profound ways. Below are compelling stories of athletes who have made significant contributions, reflecting the transformative impact of faith, community service, and chaplaincy.

---

1. Tim Tebow: A Legacy of Faith and Service

Tim Tebow, a former NFL quarterback and professional baseball player, is renowned not only for his athleticism but also for his unwavering faith and dedication to helping others.

- **Faith and Giving**: Tebow founded the Tim Tebow Foundation, which focuses on uplifting people in need through various programs. The foundation's initiatives include hosting "Night to Shine," a prom night experience for individuals with special needs, and providing free surgeries to children with life-threatening conditions.

- **Inspiration from Chaplaincy**: Tebow credits his faith and the influence of sports chaplains during his career for shaping his commitment to serving others. His work demonstrates how spiritual guidance can inspire athletes to leverage their fame for philanthropy.

2. Muhammad Ali: Championing Social Justice and Equality

While Muhammad Ali is celebrated for his boxing prowess, his contributions outside the ring are equally impactful.

- **Activism and Outreach**: Ali used his platform to advocate for civil rights, religious freedom, and global humanitarian efforts. He traveled to developing countries to deliver food, medical supplies, and support for impoverished communities.
- **Faith as a Driver**: Ali's faith as a Muslim deeply influenced his commitment to giving back, and he often credited spiritual advisors and chaplains for keeping him grounded during his career. His work highlights the role of spiritual care in motivating athletes to focus on causes larger than themselves.

3. Serena Williams: Empowering Women and Communities

Tennis legend Serena Williams has long been a role model for excellence, resilience, and philanthropy.

- **Supporting Vulnerable Groups**: Through her Serena Williams Fund, she supports education initiatives and provides resources for victims of violence. Williams has also partnered with organizations to build schools in underserved communities in Africa.
- **Chaplaincy and Faith**: Williams often speaks about her faith and the guidance she's received from spiritual mentors, which fuels her passion for creating opportunities for others.

4. Drew Brees: Rebuilding Communities

Former NFL quarterback Drew Brees has demonstrated how athletes can make tangible differences in their communities.

- **Post-Katrina Efforts**: After Hurricane Katrina devastated New Orleans, Brees played a key role in rebuilding efforts. He and his wife founded the Brees Dream Foundation, which has donated millions to improve healthcare, education, and athletic facilities in Louisiana and beyond.
- **Spiritual Influence**: Brees often credits chaplains and his Christian faith for inspiring his commitment to service, particularly in times of crisis.

5. Cristiano Ronaldo: A Global Ambassador of Generosity

Soccer superstar Cristiano Ronaldo is known for his philanthropic efforts worldwide.

- **Charitable Donations**: Ronaldo has donated millions of dollars to disaster relief efforts, hospitals, and cancer treatment centers. He has also auctioned off his personal awards to fund children's hospitals and education programs.
- **Faith-Driven Compassion**: While Ronaldo's faith is personal, he has often been seen working with community chaplains and spiritual leaders, emphasizing the importance of giving back as a moral responsibility.

6. Manny Pacquiao: Faith in Action

Manny Pacquiao, a world-famous boxer and senator in the Philippines, has dedicated much of his life to serving his country's poor and vulnerable populations.

- **Service through Faith**: Pacquiao attributes his charitable work to his Christian faith, which deepened during his boxing career. He has built homes for the homeless, funded educational programs, and provided disaster relief.
- **Role of Chaplaincy**: During his career, Pacquiao worked closely with chaplains who helped him navigate fame and focus on his faith, which he credits as the foundation of his generosity.

7. LeBron James: Investing in the Future

NBA star LeBron James is not only a basketball icon but also a champion for education and community development.

- **The "I PROMISE" School**: James launched the I PROMISE School in Akron, Ohio, for at-risk children, providing them with free tuition, meals, and college scholarships.
- **Inspiration and Faith**: James has spoken about the spiritual values instilled in him by mentors and chaplains, emphasizing that his work is driven by gratitude and a desire to uplift others.

---

8. Allyson Felix: Advocacy and Support for Mothers

Olympic sprinter Allyson Felix has used her platform to advocate for maternal health and support for women in sports.

- **Maternal Care**: After experiencing complications during her pregnancy, Felix partnered with organizations to improve maternal healthcare access for women worldwide.
- **Guided by Faith**: Felix's Christian faith and the encouragement of chaplains during her career have inspired her to focus on causes that align with her values.

Conclusion

These stories demonstrate the profound impact that athletes can have on their communities and the world when they are guided by faith, chaplaincy, and a commitment to service. By providing spiritual care, encouragement, and moral grounding, chaplains play a critical role in helping athletes recognize their potential to give back. As these examples show, the influence of faith and chaplaincy extends far beyond the game, creating ripples of positive change that benefit countless lives.

CHAPTER 08

CHALLENGES AND CONTROVERSIES – FACING ADVERSITY

The role of chaplains is vital in many contexts, including hospitals, schools, prisons, and sports. However, chaplains often encounter significant challenges and controversies in their line of work. They must navigate complex situations while providing spiritual care to diverse populations, managing their own mental and emotional well-being, and addressing societal misconceptions about their role. This chapter explores the unique challenges chaplains face, the controversies surrounding their work, and strategies to address these issues effectively.

Challenges in Chaplaincy

1. Providing Spiritual Care to Diverse Populations

Chaplains are called to serve individuals from various religious, cultural, and non-religious backgrounds. This diversity presents both an opportunity for inclusivity and a challenge to traditional chaplaincy practices.

- **Navigating Religious Differences**: Chaplains must balance respecting individual beliefs while providing meaningful spiritual care. For example, a Christian chaplain may need to provide support to a Muslim or atheist patient, requiring cultural sensitivity and an understanding of diverse spiritual needs.
- **Non-Religious Populations**: The rise of secularism has increased the demand for chaplains to offer non-religious spiritual support, such as counseling and emotional care, without relying on prayer or scripture.

2. Measuring Outcomes of Spiritual Care

One of the most persistent challenges in chaplaincy is the lack of clear evidence linking spiritual care to measurable outcomes, such as patient recovery or emotional well-being.

- **Subjective Nature of Spiritual Support**: Unlike medical treatments, the benefits of spiritual care are often subjective and difficult to quantify.
- **Need for Research**: Limited studies exist that demonstrate the impact of chaplaincy on outcomes like patient satisfaction, mental health improvement, or team morale, leading to skepticism about its value in some settings.

3. Emotional and Mental Health Risks

The demands of chaplaincy can take a toll on chaplains' mental and emotional health, particularly when they encounter traumatic situations or high levels of stress.

- **Burnout and Compassion Fatigue**: Constant exposure to grief, loss, and crises can lead to emotional exhaustion and burnout.
- **Vicarious Trauma**: Chaplains often absorb the emotional weight of those they serve, which can lead to secondary traumatic stress.

4. Vocational Vulnerabilities

Chaplains face professional challenges, including job insecurity, role ambiguity, and insufficient recognition.

- **Role Clarity**: In some organizations, the chaplain's responsibilities may overlap with those of counselors, social workers, or spiritual leaders, creating confusion and potential conflicts.
- **Job Stability**: Many chaplaincy positions are part-time or dependent on external funding, making long-term employment uncertain.

5. Misunderstandings and Stereotypes

There is often a lack of understanding about what chaplains do, both within the organizations they serve and in the broader community.

- **Stereotypes**: Chaplains are sometimes seen solely as religious figures, which can alienate individuals who do not identify with a particular faith.
- **Undervaluation**: In some settings, chaplaincy is viewed as ancillary rather than integral to the overall mission, leading to underfunding and marginalization.

Controversies in Chaplaincy

1. The Necessity of Prayer and Religious Rituals

The debate over whether chaplaincy must include prayer or religious rituals reflects broader tensions about the role of religion in public spaces.

- **Secular Chaplaincy**: Some argue that chaplains should move away from explicitly religious practices to focus on universal spiritual care.
- **Balancing Tradition and Modernity**: Others believe that chaplaincy should maintain its religious roots while adapting to contemporary needs.

2. Ethical Dilemmas

Chaplains often face ethical dilemmas, such as balancing confidentiality with organizational policies or addressing conflicting values between their faith and the needs of those they serve.

- **End-of-Life Decisions**: Chaplains may be called to support families making difficult decisions, such as withdrawing life support, which can be emotionally and ethically challenging.
- **Moral Distress**: Situations where chaplains cannot act in accordance with their beliefs can lead to personal and professional conflict.

3. Inclusivity and Representation

As chaplaincy expands to serve more diverse populations, questions about inclusivity and representation have arisen.

- **Underrepresentation**: Certain religious or non-religious groups may be underrepresented in chaplaincy, leading to calls for more inclusive hiring practices.
- **Equity in Access**: Ensuring that all individuals have access to chaplaincy services, regardless of their background, remains a significant challenge.

Chaplains as Emotional and Professional Support for Staff

Beyond serving patients or athletes, chaplains play a critical role in supporting the emotional and professional well-being of healthcare staff, coaches, and other team members.

- **Staff Care**: Chaplains provide a listening ear and emotional support to staff experiencing stress or burnout.
- **Team Building**: By fostering a sense of community and shared purpose, chaplains contribute to a more cohesive and resilient team.

Strategies for Addressing Challenges

1. **Education and Training**
   - Chaplains should receive training in cultural competency, ethics, and non-religious forms of spiritual care to better serve diverse populations.
2. **Research and Advocacy**
   - Conducting research to measure the impact of chaplaincy can strengthen its credibility and secure funding.

- o Advocating for the inclusion of chaplaincy as an essential service can enhance recognition and support.

3. **Self-Care and Peer Support**
   - o Chaplains must prioritize self-care and seek peer support to manage the emotional demands of their work.
   - o Organizations can provide resources, such as counseling or mentorship programs, to support chaplain well-being.

4. **Role Clarification**
   - o Clearly defining the chaplain's role within an organization can reduce misunderstandings and improve collaboration with other professionals.

5. **Promoting Inclusivity**
   - o Hiring chaplains from diverse backgrounds and fostering an inclusive approach to spiritual care can address concerns about representation and equity.

Conclusion

Chaplains face numerous challenges and controversies, from navigating diverse spiritual needs to addressing ethical dilemmas and ensuring their own well-being. Despite these obstacles, chaplains remain invaluable contributors to the emotional and spiritual health of the communities they serve. By embracing innovation, inclusivity, and self-care, chaplains can continue to thrive and make a profound impact in an ever-changing world.

Challenges Chaplains Face in Their Ministry

Chaplains serve as spiritual and emotional anchors for individuals navigating life's most difficult moments. However, their ministry is not without challenges. These challenges stem from the evolving nature of their work, organizational dynamics, and the personal toll it takes on their well-being. This chapter explores these challenges in detail, focusing on the complexities of commitment to recovery, the adaptation of new skills, balancing risks, organizational hurdles, and the impact of burnout.

1. Commitment to Physical and Mental Recovery in Clinical Pastoral Education (CPE)

Clinical Pastoral Education (CPE) is a foundational training for chaplains, equipping them with the skills to provide spiritual care in complex environments. However, the commitment to both physical and mental recovery in CPE poses unique challenges:

- **Intensive Training Requirements**: CPE involves rigorous academic and practical training, often in high-stress environments like hospitals or prisons. Chaplains must manage their own mental and emotional health while learning to care for others.
- **Emotional Burden**: The process of self-reflection and peer review inherent in CPE can be emotionally taxing, as chaplains must confront their biases, vulnerabilities, and limitations.
- **Physical Strain**: Long hours, irregular schedules, and the physical demands of being present for patients or clients can lead to fatigue and physical health issues.

2. Practicing New Skills in Response to Emerging Needs

The COVID-19 pandemic and other crises have required chaplains to adapt rapidly to new methods of care delivery. This adaptation has introduced challenges such as:

- **Social Distancing and Remote Care**: Chaplains have had to provide spiritual care while adhering to social distancing guidelines, which often means relying on technology such as video calls. This shift has been particularly difficult in contexts like end-of-life care, where physical presence is traditionally significant.
- **Facilitating Technology-Based Interactions**: Facilitating FaceTime or other virtual communication tools for dying patients and their families has become a new skill for chaplains. While this provides a vital connection, it lacks the depth of in-person interactions and can leave chaplains feeling ineffective or disconnected.
- **Learning Curve**: For many chaplains, integrating technology into their practice requires developing technical skills and overcoming resistance to change.

3. Balancing Instincts to Help with Personal Safety

Chaplains are often driven by an instinct to provide care and comfort to distressed individuals. However, this instinct can sometimes put them in harm's way:

- **Potential Danger**: In crisis situations, such as during violent incidents, natural disasters, or pandemics, chaplains may face physical risks. Their commitment to being present for others often leads them to prioritize the needs of those they serve over their own safety.
- **Emotional Risks**: Chaplains who immerse themselves in high-stress situations may also experience emotional repercussions, such as vicarious trauma or compassion fatigue.
- **Ethical Dilemmas**: Balancing the urge to help with the potential for harm to themselves or others can create ethical and emotional tension, making it difficult to make clear decisions in real time.

---

4. Organizational Hurdles and Other Care-Related Matters

Chaplains often navigate complex organizational dynamics that can hinder their ability to provide effective care.

- **Ambiguous Roles**: In many settings, chaplains' roles are not clearly defined, leading to misunderstandings about their purpose and contributions. This ambiguity can result in underutilization or unrealistic expectations.
- **Resource Constraints**: Limited budgets, inadequate staffing, and a lack of institutional support can make it difficult for chaplains to perform their duties effectively.
- **Interdisciplinary Tensions**: Chaplains often work alongside medical, educational, or correctional staff, which can lead to differing priorities and conflicts about the best approach to care.

- **Bureaucratic Barriers**: Navigating organizational policies and procedures can slow down or complicate the chaplain's ability to respond promptly to individuals in need.

5. High Job Demands and Low Job Resources

The imbalance between high job demands and low job resources is a significant contributor to burnout among chaplains.

- **Emotional Exhaustion**: Chaplains are often exposed to intense emotional experiences, such as grief, trauma, and despair. The cumulative impact of these experiences can lead to emotional exhaustion and detachment.
- **Burnout**: High job demands, coupled with insufficient resources like time, funding, or peer support, can lead to burnout—a state of physical, emotional, and mental exhaustion. Burnout not only affects chaplains' well-being but also their ability to provide effective care.
- **Work-Life Imbalance**: The demands of chaplaincy often extend beyond regular working hours, making it difficult for chaplains to maintain a healthy work-life balance.

Addressing the Challenges

To overcome these challenges, chaplains and the organizations they serve must adopt proactive strategies:

1. **Enhanced Training**: CPE programs should include modules on self-care, cultural competence, and the use of

technology to better prepare chaplains for modern challenges.

2. **Support Systems**: Institutions should provide mental health resources, peer support groups, and opportunities for professional development to help chaplains manage stress and avoid burnout.
3. **Role Clarification**: Clearly defining the chaplain's role within organizations can reduce misunderstandings and promote collaboration with other professionals.
4. **Advocacy for Resources**: Chaplains should advocate for adequate staffing, funding, and institutional support to ensure they can meet the demands of their work effectively.
5. **Ethical Training**: Providing chaplains with tools to navigate ethical dilemmas can help them make informed decisions that balance compassion with personal safety.

Conclusion

The challenges chaplains face in their ministry are numerous and complex, reflecting the evolving nature of their work and the diverse needs of those they serve. By addressing these challenges through training, support, and advocacy, chaplains can continue to provide meaningful spiritual care while safeguarding their own well-being. Their resilience and adaptability remain key to navigating these difficulties and ensuring the continued impact of chaplaincy in a changing world.

Addressing Controversies and Ethical Dilemmas in Sports

Sports chaplaincy exists at the intersection of spirituality, ethics, and high-performance athletics. While chaplains provide invaluable support to athletes, coaches, and teams, their involvement is often challenged by ethical dilemmas and controversies. One of the key issues is that chaplains are frequently brought into situations too late, often as a last resort rather than as proactive participants in addressing ethical challenges. This chapter explores the controversies and ethical dilemmas chaplains face in sports and offers insights into how these challenges can be addressed.

Ethical Dilemmas in Sports Chaplaincy

1. **Post-Hoc Involvement of Chaplains** Chaplains are often consulted only after crises have escalated, such as moral failures, controversies, or team conflicts. Their late involvement can limit their effectiveness in resolving ethical dilemmas and building trust.
   - **Example**: In cases of public scandals involving athletes, chaplains may only be asked to intervene after reputational damage has occurred, rather than providing preventative spiritual guidance.
   - **Implications**: This reactive approach undermines the holistic role chaplains could play in fostering ethical decision-making and spiritual resilience.
2. **Blurred Boundaries Between Roles** Chaplains may face dilemmas regarding their roles within a team or organization:
   - **Conflict of Interest**: Balancing loyalty to the team versus the spiritual and emotional well-being of individual athletes.

- o **Confidentiality**: Navigating the line between maintaining an athlete's trust and reporting issues of concern, such as substance abuse or moral failings, to leadership.

3. **Pressure to Conform to Organizational Values**
   - o Chaplains sometimes face pressure to prioritize team performance over their pastoral duties.
   - o Ethical conflicts can arise when chaplains are asked to endorse or overlook behaviors inconsistent with their spiritual values, such as unethical recruitment practices or doping.

4. **Cultural and Religious Sensitivity**
   - o Teams are often diverse, including athletes with varying cultural backgrounds and religious beliefs. Chaplains must navigate the tension between their own religious convictions and the need to respect the spiritual or secular beliefs of those they serve.
   - o **Dilemma**: Balancing inclusivity with authenticity in their ministry without alienating athletes from minority faiths or non-religious backgrounds.

5. **Handling Moral Failures**
   - o Chaplains often intervene in cases of personal misconduct, such as infidelity, substance abuse, or cheating scandals.
   - o The dilemma arises when chaplains must balance supporting the athlete's recovery with addressing the broader ethical implications of their behavior.

Controversies in Sports Chaplaincy

1. **Perceived Favoritism**
   - o Chaplains who spend more time with certain athletes or coaches may face accusations of favoritism.

- o This perception can create divisions within teams, undermining the chaplain's ability to foster unity.

2. **Secular Pushback**
   - o In secular or pluralistic organizations, the presence of a chaplain may be seen as promoting a specific religious agenda.
   - o Chaplains often face resistance from stakeholders who question the relevance or neutrality of spiritual care in sports.

3. **Overstepping Professional Boundaries**
   - o Critics argue that chaplains sometimes take on roles outside their scope, such as acting as counselors or life coaches, without appropriate training or qualifications.
   - o This can lead to questions about their professional credibility and the effectiveness of their interventions.

4. **Tokenism and Marginalization**
   - o Some organizations appoint chaplains to fulfill public relations objectives rather than to genuinely integrate spiritual care into their teams.
   - o In these cases, chaplains may feel undervalued or sidelined, limiting their ability to make meaningful contributions.

Addressing Ethical Dilemmas and Controversies

1. **Proactive Engagement**
   - o **Solution**: Chaplains should be involved in team dynamics and decision-making from the outset, rather than being called upon only in moments of crisis.

- o **Example**: Regular team meetings, ethical workshops, and one-on-one mentoring sessions can help integrate chaplaincy into the team culture.

2. **Role Clarification**
   - o Establishing clear boundaries and expectations for chaplains' roles can prevent misunderstandings and conflicts of interest.
   - o Organizations should provide formal job descriptions that define chaplains' scope of practice and ensure alignment with team values.

3. **Training in Ethics and Diversity**
   - o Chaplains should receive ongoing training in cultural competence, ethical decision-making, and conflict resolution.
   - o **Example**: Workshops on navigating multi-faith environments or dealing with issues like doping and mental health.

4. **Building Trust and Transparency**
   - o Trust is a cornerstone of effective chaplaincy. Chaplains must cultivate relationships with athletes and team leadership, ensuring open communication and confidentiality.
   - o Transparent practices, such as maintaining impartiality and adhering to professional codes of conduct, can mitigate controversies.

5. **Collaboration with Other Professionals**
   - o Chaplains should collaborate with psychologists, counselors, and medical staff to provide holistic care for athletes.
   - o **Example**: Partnering with mental health professionals to address issues like burnout or addiction.

6. **Advocacy for Inclusion**
   - o To address concerns about favoritism or tokenism, chaplains should advocate for inclusive practices that respect the diversity of team members.

- o Initiatives such as interfaith prayer services or community outreach programs can foster a sense of unity and mutual respect.

Future Directions

1. **Research and Evidence-Based Practice**
   - o More research is needed to evaluate the impact of chaplaincy on ethical decision-making, team cohesion, and athlete well-being.
   - o Evidence-based practices can strengthen the case for integrating chaplaincy into sports organizations.
2. **Ethics Committees**
   - o Establishing ethics committees within sports organizations can provide chaplains with guidance and support when navigating complex dilemmas.
3. **Community Engagement**
   - o Chaplains should extend their ministry beyond the team, engaging with local communities to promote ethical values and inspire future generations of athletes.

Conclusion

Chaplains play a crucial role in addressing the ethical dilemmas and controversies inherent in sports. By proactively engaging with teams, clarifying their roles, and embracing ongoing education, chaplains can navigate these challenges effectively. Their presence not only supports individual athletes but also fosters a culture of integrity and respect, ensuring that the values of sportsmanship and spirituality remain at the heart of athletic endeavors.

Maintaining Integrity and Faith in Difficult Situations

In the high-pressure world of sports, chaplains often face difficult situations where integrity, faith, and moral character are tested. Athletes, coaches, and other sports staff may turn to chaplains in moments of personal crisis, defeat, or ethical dilemma, and it is within these moments that a chaplain's role becomes crucial. Maintaining integrity and faith in difficult situations is not just about providing comfort; it's about upholding the principles of compassion, honesty, and spiritual guidance, while also ensuring that the athlete or individual's needs are met in a way that respects both their humanity and their faith.

The Role of Chaplains in Difficult Situations

Chaplains in sports settings often encounter a wide range of challenges and situations where maintaining integrity is essential. These include moments of moral failure, personal crisis, or professional setbacks that athletes face, such as injuries, loss, or burnout. In these circumstances, the chaplain's role becomes one of listening, comforting, praying, and offering support, while maintaining a strong sense of integrity and unwavering faith.

Key Principles for Maintaining Integrity and Faith

1. **Listening with Empathy and Compassion**
    o **Active Listening**: One of the chaplain's core skills is active listening. By giving their full attention, chaplains demonstrate respect for the person's experience, allowing them to process emotions and articulate their concerns.
    o **Non-Judgmental Presence**: Chaplains must listen without judgment, offering a safe space for individuals to express their struggles without fear of criticism or misunderstanding.
    o **Example**: An athlete grappling with a poor performance or an ethical lapse may find solace in knowing that their chaplain truly hears and acknowledges their pain. This act of listening fosters trust and allows the chaplain to offer relevant, thoughtful advice or prayer.
2. **Comforting with Compassionate Care**
    o **Spiritual Comfort**: Chaplains provide comfort by grounding individuals in faith. When athletes face challenges, whether personal or professional, chaplains can offer the assurance of divine presence, comfort, and peace.
    o **Emotional Support**: Beyond spiritual care, chaplains offer emotional support by empathizing with athletes' frustrations, fears, and disappointments. This can help alleviate the weight of adversity and provide a path toward healing.
    o **Example**: During times of injury or defeat, chaplains can remind athletes of God's love and plan, reinforcing their sense of purpose and worth, regardless of their current circumstances.
3. **Praying for Strength and Guidance**

- Faith in Action: Prayer is a central aspect of chaplaincy. Chaplains can offer prayers that bring hope, encourage perseverance, and deepen the individual's connection with God. Praying with and for athletes not only strengthens their faith but also reaffirms the chaplain's integrity in their pastoral duties.
- **Spiritual Resilience**: Through prayer, chaplains help athletes and team members find spiritual strength in the face of adversity. Prayers for healing, courage, and clarity can uplift those who are struggling with a variety of issues, from injuries to personal crises.
- **Example**: A chaplain praying with an athlete after a significant loss may focus on themes of restoration, God's peace, and the hope of new beginnings, offering not just comfort but a renewed sense of spiritual purpose.

4. Supporting Through Guidance and Accountability

- **Ethical Guidance**: Chaplains offer guidance based on biblical principles, helping athletes navigate moral and ethical dilemmas. This support is particularly critical when athletes are faced with decisions that challenge their integrity, such as substance abuse, cheating, or other forms of misconduct.
- **Accountability Partners**: Chaplains can serve as accountability partners, helping athletes to remain true to their values and beliefs, particularly when the pressures of the sports world tempt them to compromise their principles.
- **Example**: When an athlete struggles with temptation or a personal moral lapse, the chaplain can guide them toward self-reflection, repentance, and the restoration of their relationship with both God and the team.

Maintaining Integrity in the Midst of Adversity

1. **Remaining True to Personal Beliefs**
2. Chaplains in sports settings often face challenges where their beliefs are tested. For example, they may be asked to condone behavior or endorse practices that conflict with their personal faith or values. In such situations, chaplains must remain true to their beliefs while still providing care and support. This requires both courage and compassion to navigate complex situations without compromising on integrity.
   - **Example**: If an athlete is involved in unethical behavior, a chaplain may offer loving, but firm guidance to the athlete, helping them reconcile their actions with their faith without endorsing or accepting the behavior.
3. **Setting Boundaries with Grace**
4. Chaplains must also set clear boundaries between their spiritual role and the expectations of the team or organization. In some cases, athletes or staff may push for personal favors or actions that overstep the chaplain's role as a spiritual caregiver. Chaplains must be able to assert these boundaries with grace and clarity, ensuring that their ministry remains focused on spiritual guidance and well-being.
   - **Example**: If an athlete asks a chaplain to help cover up a misconduct or moral failing, the chaplain must refuse to condone such actions, gently but firmly reinforcing the importance of honesty and integrity while continuing to provide spiritual and emotional support.
5. **Managing Stress and Burnout**
6. Chaplains also face their own challenges of stress, burnout, and emotional exhaustion. The demands of

supporting athletes in high-stakes, emotionally charged environments can take a toll. Chaplains must prioritize self-care, regularly seeking spiritual renewal, rest, and professional development to ensure that they can continue to serve effectively.

  o **Example**: A chaplain may need to take time for personal reflection and prayer to renew their own faith and strength, so they can return to their duties with clarity and renewed purpose.

Practical Strategies for Maintaining Integrity and Faith

1. **Regular Reflection and Prayer**
2. Chaplains should make regular time for personal reflection, prayer, and study of scripture to remain grounded in their own faith. This practice not only supports their personal growth but equips them to provide the spiritual care needed by athletes and team members.
3. **Mentorship and Peer Support**
4. Chaplains should seek out mentorship and peer support from other experienced chaplains or clergy. This network provides a source of accountability and encouragement, helping chaplains maintain their integrity in difficult situations.
5. **Continued Education and Training**
6. Professional development, including ethical training and cultural competence, equips chaplains to handle diverse challenges in a respectful and effective manner. This ongoing learning ensures chaplains are

prepared to meet the evolving needs of athletes and sports teams.

Conclusion

In difficult situations, chaplains play a crucial role in maintaining integrity and faith, both for themselves and for those they serve. By listening attentively, offering comfort, praying for strength, and providing ongoing support, chaplains uphold the values of compassion, ethical responsibility, and spiritual resilience. Their ability to maintain their integrity in challenging circumstances not only helps athletes and teams navigate personal crises but also strengthens their own spiritual resolve, enabling them to continue serving as a beacon of faith and hope in the demanding world of sports.

CHAPTER 09

STORIES OF TRANSFORMATION

Impactful Transformations through Chaplaincy

The role of chaplains in sports extends far beyond spiritual care during games or personal crises; it is a ministry that fosters profound and lasting transformation. These transformations occur not only within individual athletes but also across teams and communities, shaping lives in ways that transcend the boundaries of sports. This chapter highlights real stories of how chaplaincy has brought about impactful transformations in the lives of athletes, coaches, and their wider communities.

1. An Athlete's Journey from Anguish to Faith

The Challenge:

John, a professional football player, experienced a career-altering injury during a critical game. The injury left him feeling hopeless and disconnected from his purpose, as he grappled with the sudden possibility of early retirement.

The Chaplain's Role:

The team's chaplain approached John with unwavering support. Through active listening, empathetic counsel, and shared prayer sessions, the chaplain helped him confront his fears and explore his faith as a source of strength.

The Transformation:

With the chaplain's encouragement, John began to view his injury not as an end, but as a new beginning. He enrolled in a sports management program, transitioned into coaching, and became an advocate for young athletes dealing with setbacks. He attributes his transformation to the chaplain's guidance and God's grace, calling it the "spiritual turning point" of his life.

---

2. Rebuilding a Team's Unity

The Challenge:

A basketball team, once celebrated for its camaraderie, fell into disarray due to internal conflicts and a losing streak. Divisive behavior among teammates caused morale to plummet, threatening the team's performance and spirit.

The Chaplain's Role:

The team chaplain initiated group sessions focused on forgiveness, communication, and shared purpose. Using biblical principles of unity and love, the chaplain facilitated honest conversations and led team-building exercises that emphasized mutual respect and collaboration.

The Transformation:

The team experienced a remarkable turnaround, not just in their performance but also in their relationships. They embraced a renewed sense of brotherhood, openly crediting the chaplain for helping them reconnect with each other and their shared faith. Their season concluded with a winning streak, but more importantly, a bond that extended beyond the court.

---

3. A Coach's Redemption

The Challenge:

Coach Sarah, a highly driven leader, faced widespread criticism after a public scandal involving her temper during a game. The incident alienated her from her players and tarnished her reputation, leaving her struggling with guilt and a sense of failure.

The Chaplain's Role:

The team chaplain reached out to Sarah privately, offering pastoral care and a safe space to process her emotions. Through scripture study and prayer, the chaplain helped her rediscover her values and develop strategies for leading with humility and grace.

The Transformation:

Sarah publicly apologized to her team and the community, acknowledging her mistakes and committing to change. She began mentoring young coaches, sharing her journey as a lesson in redemption and personal growth. The experience deepened her faith and reshaped her leadership style, earning her respect and admiration anew.

---

4. A Community Uplifted by a Chaplain's Vision

The Challenge:

In a low-income neighborhood plagued by limited opportunities, many young athletes faced systemic barriers that hindered their potential. Sports became an outlet, but the absence of mentorship left these young talents vulnerable to negative influences.

The Chaplain's Role:

A local sports chaplain launched a community initiative, organizing after-school programs that combined athletic training with life skills and faith-based mentoring. The chaplain also connected with local churches and organizations to secure resources for scholarships and career development workshops.

The Transformation:

Dozens of young athletes from the community not only excelled in sports but also pursued higher education and meaningful careers. The chaplain's vision transformed the neighborhood into a hub of hope and inspiration, fostering a generation of leaders who now give back to their community.

---

5. A Family Reunited Through Sports Ministry

The Challenge:

Mark, a star soccer player, was estranged from his parents due to years of unresolved conflict. The strain in their relationship affected his mental health and performance on the field.

The Chaplain's Role:

Recognizing the impact of Mark's family issues, the team chaplain offered counseling to him and his parents. By facilitating open communication and using faith-based teachings on forgiveness and reconciliation, the chaplain helped them navigate their differences and heal past wounds.

The Transformation:

Mark's reconciliation with his parents brought newfound peace and focus to his life, which reflected in his game. He went on to lead his team to victory in a major championship, attributing his personal and professional triumph to the chaplain's mediation and spiritual support.

Conclusion

These stories of transformation underscore the profound impact chaplaincy can have in the realm of sports. By offering spiritual care, guidance, and unwavering support, chaplains become agents of change, helping individuals and communities overcome adversity and achieve their fullest potential. The common thread in all these stories is the chaplains' commitment to being present, fostering faith, and empowering others to navigate life's challenges with resilience and hope.

Their work, though often unseen, leaves an indelible mark on the hearts and lives they touch, proving that the ministry of chaplaincy goes far beyond the game—it transforms lives.

Testimonies of Athletes Whose Lives Were Changed Through Chaplaincy

Chaplains play an integral role in the spiritual, emotional, and personal development of athletes. Their presence provides a grounding influence, helping athletes navigate the unique challenges of sports and life. This chapter features real

testimonies of athletes whose lives were transformed through
the ministry and support of chaplains.

---

1. "Finding Peace in the Storm"

Athlete: Emily Johnson, Professional Tennis Player

*"I was at the peak of my career, winning championships and
making headlines, but inside I felt empty. I battled anxiety and
sleepless nights, terrified of losing my ranking. When the team
chaplain first approached me, I was skeptical. But his calm
presence and willingness to listen made me open up about my
struggles.*

*"Through our conversations, he introduced me to scriptures
about peace and trust in God. He reminded me that my worth
wasn't tied to my wins or losses. For the first time, I felt a
weight lift. The chaplain didn't just help me as an athlete; he
helped me rediscover myself as a person.*

*"Today, I still face challenges, but I approach them with faith
and confidence. The chaplain's guidance gave me the tools to
cope, not just in sports but in life."*

---

2. "Rebuilding After the Fall"

Athlete: Marcus Lee, Retired Football Quarterback

"I suffered a career-ending injury at 28, and my world came crashing down. My identity had been so tied to being a professional football player that I didn't know who I was without it. I fell into depression, pushing everyone away.

"The team chaplain didn't give up on me. He visited me weekly, encouraging me to talk, even when I didn't want to. He shared stories from the Bible about resilience and purpose, and slowly, I started to believe that my life wasn't over.

"With his help, I found a new purpose. I became a coach for a youth football team, mentoring kids the way he mentored me. The chaplain's patience and faith in me gave me hope when I had none. He saved my life."

---

3. "From Anger to Forgiveness"

Athlete: Sarah Blake, Professional Basketball Player

"I had a difficult relationship with my father, and that anger seeped into every part of my life, including my performance on the court. I was aggressive, short-tempered, and isolated from my teammates.

"During a team retreat, the chaplain spoke about forgiveness. It was like he was talking directly to me. I approached him afterward, and we began weekly sessions where he helped me process my feelings and find the courage to reconcile with my dad.

"That conversation changed everything. My father and I are rebuilding our relationship, and my teammates say they see a different side of me now. I owe so much to the chaplain for helping me let go of my anger and find peace."

---

4. "Faith Through Adversity"

Athlete: David Martinez, Olympic Sprinter

"I was devastated after being disqualified from a major competition due to an injury. The physical pain was nothing compared to the disappointment of not representing my country. I felt like I had let everyone down.

"The chaplain reminded me that God's plan is bigger than any race. He prayed with me and encouraged me to focus on my recovery, not just physically but spiritually. He shared verses about endurance and perseverance that became my lifeline.

"A year later, I qualified for another championship and won. But even more than the victory, I valued the spiritual strength I had gained. The chaplain taught me to trust God's timing, and that lesson has stayed with me ever since."

---

5. "A New Perspective on Success"

Athlete: Rachel Carter, Collegiate Soccer Player

"In college, I was obsessed with being the best, often at the expense of my mental health and relationships. The chaplain at our university challenged me to redefine success, not as winning but as giving my best and honoring God through my efforts.

"His mentorship changed my perspective. I started playing with joy again, focusing on being a good teammate rather than just a top scorer. That year, our team won the championship, but what mattered most to me was the sense of peace and fulfillment I found.

"The chaplain didn't just help me become a better athlete; he helped me become a better person."

---

6. "Healing a Team Divided"

Athlete: Jordan Brown, Team Captain of a Rugby Squad

"Our team was falling apart due to internal conflicts and poor communication. The chaplain stepped in, organizing group discussions and prayer sessions. He emphasized unity, drawing parallels between teamwork and biblical principles of love and fellowship.

"His efforts brought us back together, not just as teammates but as brothers. The chaplain's influence was the turning point for our season, and we went on to win the championship. But more importantly, we became a family again."

Conclusion

The testimonies in this chapter illustrate the profound impact chaplaincy has on the lives of athletes. By providing spiritual guidance, emotional support, and a steady presence, chaplains help athletes navigate the highs and lows of their careers. These stories are a testament to the transformative power of faith and compassion, underscoring why chaplaincy is an essential aspect of the sports world.

Spiritual Awakenings and Life-Altering Decisions

Athletes often find themselves at critical crossroads in their careers and lives, where spiritual awakenings can lead to transformative changes. These moments of clarity, faith, and divine intervention enable athletes to make decisions that reshape their paths, both professionally and personally. This chapter explores the profound ways spiritual awakenings influence athletes and how chaplaincy plays a vital role in these life-altering decisions.

1. Spiritual Awakening Through Adversity

Athlete: Michael Harris, Professional Baseball Player

Michael's career was derailed by a devastating injury during a pivotal game. As he struggled with the uncertainty of his future, he found himself questioning his purpose. The team chaplain reached out to him during this difficult time, introducing him to the story of Job from the Bible.

_"I realized that my worth wasn't in my stats or my career but in being a child of God," Michael shared. Inspired by this spiritual awakening, Michael transitioned into a new role as a mentor for young athletes, teaching them resilience and faith.

---

2. A Life-Altering Decision to Forgive

Athlete: Samantha Reed, Marathon Runner

Samantha carried the weight of bitterness after a public feud with a fellow competitor. The negativity affected her performance and mental health. During a post-race chapel session, the chaplain spoke about the power of forgiveness.

_"Something clicked in me that day," Samantha recalled. "I realized I was imprisoning myself with my anger." She reached out to her competitor to reconcile, a decision that brought her peace and reignited her passion for running.

---

3. Leaving Fame for Faith

Athlete: Brian Lopez, Professional Soccer Player

At the peak of his career, Brian felt an unshakable emptiness. Despite his fame and wealth, he longed for a deeper sense of purpose. A conversation with his team chaplain about the call to serve others became a turning point.

_"I prayed about it, and I knew I had to walk away," Brian said. He retired early to become a missionary, dedicating his life to spreading faith in underserved communities. His decision shocked fans but inspired many to reevaluate their priorities.

4. Rediscovering Purpose After Loss

Athlete: Rachel Adams, Collegiate Swimmer

Rachel was devastated when she narrowly missed qualifying for the Olympics. Consumed by disappointment, she isolated herself from her team and loved ones. The chaplain at her university persistently reached out, sharing scriptures about God's plan and purpose.

_"One day, he told me that failure doesn't define me—God does," Rachel said. Her spiritual awakening led her to start a nonprofit for young swimmers, focusing on character development and faith.

5. A Career Change Inspired by Faith

Athlete: Chris Evans, Retired Basketball Player

Chris's career ended abruptly due to a knee injury. Facing an identity crisis, he turned to the team chaplain, who guided him through prayer and reflection. During these sessions, Chris discovered a passion for coaching.

_"My chaplain showed me that God closes one door to open another," Chris explained. He now coaches at a high school, incorporating faith into his leadership style.

---

6. Spiritual Strength in Facing Tragedy

Athlete: Olivia Brooks, Track and Field Star

After losing her father to cancer, Olivia struggled to cope with grief while maintaining her athletic career. The team chaplain became a source of comfort, introducing her to Psalms of lament and hope.

_"Through faith, I found the strength to keep going," Olivia said. Her spiritual awakening led her to use her platform to raise awareness for cancer research and inspire others to find solace in God.

The Role of Chaplaincy in Spiritual Awakenings

Chaplains serve as guides during these transformative moments, helping athletes navigate spiritual discoveries and apply them to life-changing decisions. Their compassionate presence provides a safe space for athletes to reflect, pray, and seek divine wisdom.

By facilitating these spiritual awakenings, chaplains help athletes uncover new purposes, rebuild broken relationships, and approach life with renewed faith. These moments of clarity often ripple beyond individual lives, impacting families, communities, and even the broader world of sports.

Conclusion

Spiritual awakenings and life-altering decisions are not just pivotal moments for athletes but also testaments to the power of faith in action. With the guidance of chaplains, these athletes find strength, purpose, and direction, showing that spiritual growth is as essential to their journey as physical and mental training. These stories remind us that behind every athlete is a soul seeking meaning, and chaplaincy provides the path to finding it.

Inspirational Stories of Redemption and Growth

The world of sports is often marked by moments of triumph and adversity. However, the most compelling narratives emerge from the stories of redemption and personal growth, where athletes overcome failures, hardships, and personal flaws to become stronger, wiser, and more faith-driven individuals. These stories highlight the transformative power of chaplaincy in guiding athletes through their journeys of restoration.

---

1. The Redemption of Daniel Carter: A Second Chance at Life

Daniel Carter, a rising football star, found his promising career spiraling downward due to substance abuse and reckless behavior. After being suspended from his team, he hit rock bottom.

The team chaplain reached out to Daniel, offering a listening ear and spiritual guidance. Through a series of counseling sessions and prayer, the chaplain introduced him to the concept of grace and redemption.

_"I realized I wasn't beyond saving," Daniel shared. "God's grace gave me the courage to seek help." He entered a rehabilitation program and later returned to the sport, becoming a mentor to young athletes struggling with similar issues. Today, Daniel is celebrated not only for his comeback but also for his commitment to helping others.

---

2. From Anger to Forgiveness: Sarah Thompson's Journey

Sarah Thompson, a professional tennis player, was known for her fiery temper on the court. After a public outburst during a major tournament, she faced widespread criticism and a hefty fine.

In her lowest moment, the chaplain at her training facility approached her, sharing teachings on forgiveness and self-control. With guidance, Sarah began to confront the deeper insecurities fueling her anger.

_"Learning to forgive myself and others transformed my perspective," Sarah said. Her growth was evident in her improved demeanor both on and off the court. She now advocates for emotional health and spirituality in sports.

---

3. James Morales: Rebuilding Faith After Betrayal

James Morales, a star basketball player, faced betrayal when his closest friend and teammate leaked sensitive information about him to the media. The scandal damaged James's reputation and left him feeling bitter and isolated.

The team chaplain encouraged James to seek solace in faith and focus on forgiveness. Through scripture and prayer, James found the strength to let go of resentment and rebuild his life.

_"Forgiveness doesn't excuse their behavior, but it sets me free," James reflected. He returned to the game with renewed focus, and his humility and resilience inspired his teammates.

4. Maria Lopez: Rising Above Injury

Maria Lopez was an Olympic hopeful in gymnastics until a severe injury shattered her dreams. Devastated, she questioned her identity and purpose beyond the sport.

Her chaplain became a source of comfort and wisdom during her recovery. Through shared devotionals and conversations about God's plan, Maria found a new path.

_"I realized my purpose wasn't just gymnastics but inspiring others," Maria said. She became a coach, emphasizing character-building and faith in her training. Her story of perseverance has touched countless lives.

---

5. Redemption Through Service: Kyle Jenkins' Transformation

Kyle Jenkins, a talented but arrogant soccer player, alienated his teammates with his selfish attitude. After being benched for poor sportsmanship, Kyle was forced to confront his behavior.

A chaplain-led team retreat focused on humility and teamwork became the turning point for Kyle. Inspired by stories of servant leadership, he began volunteering in his community and prioritizing his team's success over personal glory.

_"It wasn't just about winning anymore; it was about making a difference," Kyle shared. His transformation united his team and led them to a championship victory, earning him newfound respect.

6. From Tragedy to Triumph: Olivia Green's Mission

Olivia Green, a track and field athlete, lost her mother in a tragic accident just weeks before a national competition. Overwhelmed with grief, Olivia considered quitting the sport entirely.

Her chaplain walked alongside her, providing emotional and spiritual support. Through prayer and scripture, Olivia found the strength to honor her mother's memory by continuing her journey.

_"I ran that race not for myself but for her and for God," Olivia said. She won the competition and dedicated her victory to her mother, using her platform to inspire others to overcome loss with faith.

The Role of Chaplaincy in Redemption and Growth

Chaplains serve as mentors, confidants, and spiritual guides during athletes' most vulnerable moments. Their role extends beyond the field, offering athletes a safe space to explore their struggles and rediscover their purpose. By fostering personal growth and spiritual renewal, chaplains help athletes transform their lives and positively impact others.

Conclusion

These stories of redemption and growth remind us that adversity can be a powerful catalyst for change. With the compassionate support of chaplains, athletes find strength in their faith to overcome challenges, rebuild their lives, and inspire those around them. Each narrative is a testament to the resilience of the human spirit and the transformative power of grace, proving that no setback is insurmountable with faith and determination.

CHAPTER 10

THE FUTURE OF SPORTS CHAPLAINCY

Evolving Role of Chaplains

Sports chaplaincy has become an integral part of the athletic experience, offering spiritual care, emotional support, and guidance to athletes navigating the complexities of their careers and lives. As the field continues to develop, the evolving roles of chaplains reflect broader societal changes, increased demands on athletes, and growing recognition of the importance of holistic well-being. This chapter explores the future of sports chaplaincy, focusing on its evolving roles, challenges, and opportunities.

1. The Current Role of Sports Chaplains

At its core, sports chaplaincy revolves around pastoral care—providing spiritual and emotional support to athletes, coaches, and staff. Chaplains are shepherds who walk alongside athletes, offering prayers, encouragement, and counsel during pivotal moments.

The role often includes:

- **Providing Pastoral Care:** Assisting athletes in coping with pressure, setbacks, and personal challenges.
- **Fostering Community:** Creating a sense of belonging through prayer huddles, team devotions, and shared rituals.
- **Encouraging Holistic Development:** Supporting athletes in their physical, emotional, mental, and spiritual growth.
- **Promoting Ethical Conduct:** Instilling values such as integrity, sportsmanship, and respect.

While these roles remain foundational, sports chaplaincy must adapt to changing environments to stay relevant and effective.

2. The Evolving Needs of Athletes

Athletes today face increasing demands, including:

- **Mental Health Challenges:** High-performance sports often lead to stress, anxiety, and depression.
- **Career Uncertainty:** Athletes face pressures from short careers and the need to plan for life after sports.
- **Cultural and Religious Diversity:** Athletes come from varied backgrounds, requiring chaplains to be culturally sensitive and inclusive.
- **Digital Distraction:** The pervasive influence of social media and technology presents new challenges for focus and identity.

To address these needs, sports chaplains must broaden their expertise and adapt their approaches, moving beyond traditional pastoral roles to include counseling, mentorship, and advocacy.

3. Expanding the Role of Sports Chaplains

A. *Mental Health Advocacy*

With mental health taking center stage in sports discourse, chaplains can play a critical role by:

- Partnering with psychologists to provide comprehensive care.
- Offering a safe space for athletes to express vulnerabilities.
- Helping athletes integrate faith-based practices like prayer and meditation for mental resilience.

B. *Life Transition Support*

As athletes transition out of active sports, chaplains can assist by:

- Helping them redefine their purpose and identity.
- Connecting them with career opportunities and networks.
- Offering spiritual guidance during periods of uncertainty and loss.

C. *Building Cultural Competency*

To serve diverse teams effectively, chaplains must:

- Gain knowledge of various religious and cultural traditions.
- Foster an environment of respect and inclusivity.
- Adapt rituals and practices to reflect the needs of all athletes.

D. Advocacy for Ethical Conduct

Chaplains can be role models for ethical behavior by:

- Promoting fair play and integrity in sports.
- Addressing issues like doping, cheating, and unsportsmanlike behavior.
- Encouraging athletes to be ambassadors of positive values.

---

4. Challenges Facing Sports Chaplaincy

A. Role Ambiguity

Some chaplains struggle to define their place within the team, particularly when overlapping with counselors, coaches, or managers. Clear role descriptions and training can help address this issue.

B. Funding and Support

Many chaplaincy programs rely on limited funding or voluntary efforts, restricting their reach and effectiveness. Increased investment from sports organizations and partnerships with faith-based institutions could provide sustainability.

C. Balancing Secular and Spiritual Needs

As sports environments grow more secular, chaplains must navigate the balance between providing spiritual care and respecting non-religious perspectives.

D. Accountability and Professional Standards

Establishing standardized training, certifications, and ethical guidelines is essential to maintain the credibility and professionalism of sports chaplaincy.

---

5. Opportunities for Growth

A. Integration into Sports Organizations

As the benefits of chaplaincy become more evident, sports organizations may integrate chaplains into their core support teams, offering them a formalized role in athlete development.

B. Technological Innovations

Chaplains can harness technology to:

- Provide virtual counseling and devotions.
- Create digital communities for athletes to connect and share.
- Use apps and platforms for faith-based content and mental health tools.

C. Global Expansion

With the globalization of sports, chaplaincy has opportunities to expand into underserved regions, fostering international networks and collaborations.

D. Research and Evidence-Based Practice

Conducting research on the impact of chaplaincy will provide data-driven insights, helping to refine practices and demonstrate its value to stakeholders.

---

6. Existing Literature and Practitioner Insights

Research on sports chaplaincy has largely focused on anecdotal evidence from practitioners working with elite athletes. Studies have highlighted the importance of:

- The chaplain's "ministry of presence" as a source of comfort and stability.
- The chaplain's role in fostering a sense of community and team spirit.
- The integration of spiritual practices into athlete routines, enhancing focus and resilience.

However, more empirical research is needed to quantify outcomes and advocate for greater inclusion of chaplaincy in sports organizations.

7. The Vision for the Future

The future of sports chaplaincy lies in its ability to adapt and innovate while staying true to its mission of serving athletes holistically. Key priorities for the coming years include:

- Establishing chaplaincy as an essential service in sports.
- Providing specialized training in mental health, cultural competency, and life transition counseling.
- Advocating for chaplaincy's role in shaping ethical and spiritually grounded athletes.

Conclusion

The evolving role of chaplains reflects the dynamic needs of the sports world. By embracing change, addressing challenges, and seizing opportunities, sports chaplaincy can continue to make a profound impact on the lives of athletes and their communities. This holistic approach to care ensures that chaplains remain indispensable in fostering resilience, faith, and purpose in the competitive arena and beyond.

The Future Landscape of Sports Chaplaincy

The future of sports chaplaincy is shaped by evolving societal, cultural, and professional dynamics that demand adaptability and innovation. As athletes increasingly seek holistic care that nurtures their physical, emotional, mental, and spiritual well-being, the landscape of sports chaplaincy must expand to meet these needs. This chapter examines emerging trends, challenges, and opportunities in sports chaplaincy, envisioning its growth and impact in the coming decades.

---

1. The Expanding Role of Sports Chaplains

Traditionally, sports chaplaincy has focused on providing spiritual and emotional support. However, the scope of this role is expanding to include more integrated care that addresses diverse aspects of an athlete's life. Key trends include:

A. Mental Health and Emotional Resilience

- **Increased Mental Health Awareness:** Athletes face intense pressure to perform, leading to heightened awareness of mental health challenges such as anxiety, depression, and burnout.
- **Holistic Care Integration:** Chaplains will increasingly collaborate with mental health professionals to provide comprehensive support, blending spiritual guidance with psychological care.
- **Proactive Resilience Building:** Training athletes to use spiritual practices for emotional resilience, such as meditation, prayer, and mindfulness.

B. Diversity and Inclusion

- **Serving Multifaith and Secular Groups:** Chaplains must adapt to serve teams with diverse religious beliefs or no faith affiliations, fostering inclusive environments.

- **Cultural Competency Training:** Developing an understanding of different cultural and spiritual traditions to build trust and respect within diverse teams.

C. Career and Life Transition Support

- **Beyond Active Sports:** Chaplains will play a critical role in helping athletes transition from competitive sports to post-career opportunities, addressing identity loss, and redefining purpose.
- **Work-Life Balance:** Guiding athletes to achieve balance between their professional commitments and personal lives.

2. The Integration of Technology in Chaplaincy

As technology transforms the way we communicate and interact, chaplaincy must evolve to incorporate digital tools that enhance accessibility and effectiveness.

A. Virtual Chaplaincy Services

- Online counseling and spiritual support platforms to reach athletes during travel or isolation.
- Virtual devotionals, prayer groups, and meditative practices to maintain connectivity and community.

B. Digital Resources

- Development of apps providing faith-based content, inspirational messages, and guided meditations tailored for athletes.
- Podcasts and videos that offer spiritual insights, practical advice, and encouragement for athletes.

C. Data-Driven Insights

- Using technology to track and assess the impact of chaplaincy programs, gathering data on athlete well-being and program outcomes.

3. Institutional Support and Professionalization

To secure a sustainable future, sports chaplaincy must gain stronger institutional backing and develop professional standards.

A. Organizational Integration

- Embedding chaplains within sports organizations as key members of the support team.
- Offering chaplaincy services as part of athlete wellness programs.

B. Training and Certification

- Establishing standardized training programs to ensure chaplains are equipped to address modern challenges.

- Certification processes to formalize the role and enhance credibility within the sports industry.

C. Funding and Resources

- Securing financial support from sports organizations, faith-based groups, and community stakeholders to expand chaplaincy services.
- Developing partnerships with universities and training centers to build the next generation of sports chaplains.

---

4. Challenges Shaping the Future

While the opportunities for growth are significant, sports chaplaincy faces challenges that must be addressed to remain relevant and impactful.

A. Secularization of Sports

- Balancing the spiritual focus of chaplaincy with secular values in modern sports.
- Ensuring chaplaincy services are inclusive and appealing to all, regardless of religious affiliation.

B. Burnout Among Chaplains

- High demands and emotional tolls can lead to burnout. Future programs must prioritize the well-being of chaplains themselves.
- Providing mental health resources and peer support networks for chaplains.

C. Ethical and Professional Boundaries

- Navigating ethical dilemmas, such as conflicts of interest, while maintaining trust and integrity.
- Establishing clear boundaries between spiritual care and counseling to avoid overstepping professional roles.

5. Opportunities for Global Expansion

The globalization of sports presents new opportunities for chaplaincy to make an impact across cultures and regions.

A. Serving Underserved Regions

- Expanding chaplaincy services to developing countries where athletes may lack access to spiritual and emotional care.
- Training local chaplains to ensure culturally relevant and sustainable programs.

B. Building International Networks

- Connecting chaplains across the globe to share best practices, resources, and strategies.
- Hosting international conferences and workshops to advance the field of sports chaplaincy.

6. Envisioning the Future

The future landscape of sports chaplaincy will be defined by its ability to adapt and innovate while staying true to its mission of service. Key goals for the field include:

- **Holistic Athlete Care:** Prioritizing the physical, mental, emotional, and spiritual dimensions of athlete well-being.
- **Increased Visibility:** Raising awareness about the value of chaplaincy through research, advocacy, and storytelling.
- **Global Impact:** Expanding chaplaincy's reach to underserved communities and fostering international collaboration.
- **Sustainability:** Building robust support systems to ensure chaplaincy thrives in the long term.

Conclusion

As sports evolve, so too must chaplaincy. The future of sports chaplaincy lies in its capacity to meet the complex needs of athletes while navigating societal changes and professional challenges. By embracing innovation, fostering inclusivity, and maintaining its spiritual foundation, sports chaplaincy will continue to be a transformative force, enriching the lives of athletes and the communities they serve.

Innovations and New Approaches in Sports Chaplaincy Ministry

The ministry of sports chaplaincy, like many forms of pastoral care, is evolving to meet the changing needs of athletes, sports teams, and organizations. As the world of sports becomes more globalized, diverse, and digitally connected, sports chaplains are exploring new and innovative approaches to provide spiritual support. This chapter explores these emerging trends and practices, highlighting how innovation is reshaping the landscape of sports chaplaincy.

1. Technological Integration in Chaplaincy

The rise of digital technology is transforming nearly every field, and sports chaplaincy is no exception. Chaplains are increasingly leveraging digital platforms to extend their reach, connect with athletes, and provide spiritual care in ways that were previously unimaginable.

A. Virtual Chaplaincy Services

- **Online Counseling and Support:** With the advent of video conferencing tools, chaplains can now provide real-time support to athletes, even when they are traveling or competing internationally. Virtual chaplaincy offers athletes the flexibility to seek guidance, prayer, and emotional support no matter where they are.
- **Social Media Presence:** Chaplains are using platforms like Instagram, Twitter, and YouTube to share inspirational messages, motivational scriptures, and reflections. These platforms allow chaplains to engage with a wider audience, reaching athletes beyond their immediate teams or clubs.
- **Spiritual Wellness Apps:** Some chaplains are developing or partnering with apps designed to guide athletes through spiritual practices such as prayer, meditation, or reflection. These apps can provide daily spiritual nourishment, promote mental resilience, and offer personalized support for athletes' unique challenges.

B. *Digital Retreats and Workshops*

- **Webinars and Online Workshops:** Chaplains are hosting online retreats, workshops, and seminars that address topics such as spiritual resilience, career transitions, mental health, and work-life balance. These virtual events provide athletes with practical tools and spiritual resources they can use throughout their careers and personal lives.
- **Interactive Online Groups:** Chaplains are creating virtual support groups where athletes can come together to share experiences, pray, and support each other in a safe, confidential environment.

---

2. Holistic Athlete Care: Fostering Mind, Body, and Spirit

While the physical and mental demands of sports are well-documented, chaplains are increasingly recognizing the need to support athletes in a more holistic manner—focusing not just on their spiritual lives but on their overall well-being.

A. *Collaboration with Mental Health Professionals*

- **Integrated Support Networks:** Chaplains are working closely with mental health professionals, including psychologists, counselors, and wellness coaches, to create a more comprehensive support system for athletes. This collaboration ensures that athletes receive both spiritual guidance and psychological care when dealing with challenges such as depression, anxiety, or stress.
- **Mental Health First Aid Training:** Many sports chaplains are receiving specialized training in mental health first aid

to better identify, understand, and address mental health crises among athletes. By recognizing warning signs and offering immediate support, chaplains play a pivotal role in the early intervention and prevention of more serious issues.

B. Resilience and Performance Enhancement

- **Mindfulness and Meditation:** Incorporating mindfulness and meditation into spiritual care routines is another growing trend. Chaplains are teaching athletes how to use these techniques to manage stress, enhance focus, and cultivate inner peace before, during, and after games. These practices help athletes build resilience, which is essential for maintaining peak performance in high-pressure environments.
- **Spiritual Coaching for Personal Growth:** Some chaplains now act as spiritual coaches, helping athletes navigate both their professional careers and personal growth. This includes guiding athletes on purpose, values, leadership, and overcoming adversity—offering a faith-based perspective on the challenges they face both on and off the field.

3. Expanding Chaplaincy Beyond Professional Sports

While sports chaplaincy has traditionally been focused on elite athletes and professional teams, new innovations are bringing chaplaincy to a wider range of athletes, including those at the amateur, collegiate, and grassroots levels.

A. College and University Chaplaincy

- **Campus Ministry Programs:** Chaplains are playing an increasingly important role in collegiate sports, providing not only spiritual support but also mentorship and guidance to student-athletes who are balancing academics, athletics, and personal development. University chaplains also offer resources to help athletes navigate the pressures of competition, mental health issues, and the challenges of transitioning to life after college sports.
- **Faith-Based Student Athlete Groups:** Some chaplains are fostering the development of faith-based groups on campus, where student-athletes can come together for fellowship, prayer, and encouragement. These groups provide a community where athletes can bond over shared values and experiences, helping them stay grounded in their faith while navigating the challenges of college athletics.

B. Grassroots and Community Sports

- **Community Outreach and Mentorship:** Chaplains are expanding their role in grassroots and community-level sports, offering support to youth athletes, coaches, and families. By engaging with younger generations, chaplains provide mentorship and guidance that extends beyond the field, teaching values such as integrity, respect, and perseverance.
- **Faith-Based Sports Camps:** Some chaplains have developed sports camps where youth athletes not only receive training and coaching but also have the opportunity to explore their faith through prayer, worship, and Bible study. These camps foster both athletic development and spiritual growth, creating a holistic environment for young athletes.

4. Specialized Training and Professional Development for Chaplains

To keep up with the evolving demands of sports chaplaincy, there is a growing emphasis on specialized training and professional development for chaplains.

A. Certification and Accreditation

- **Formalized Training Programs:** Sports chaplains are increasingly required to undergo formal training programs and certification processes that equip them with the knowledge and skills necessary to provide effective care in the unique environment of sports. These programs often focus on ethical considerations, mental health awareness, conflict resolution, and cross-cultural competency.
- **Ongoing Professional Development:** Sports chaplains are encouraged to continue their education and participate in ongoing professional development. This might include attending conferences, workshops, and seminars where they can share experiences, learn new techniques, and discuss best practices.

B. Expanding Leadership Roles

- **Becoming Integral Team Members:** Chaplains are being integrated more fully into team environments, taking on leadership roles in team culture development, performance optimization, and athlete well-being. By gaining the trust of athletes, chaplains are seen as valuable team members who contribute not only to the spiritual life of the team but also to the overall health and success of the organization.

5. The Future of Sports Chaplaincy: New Frontiers

Looking forward, sports chaplaincy is set to evolve and expand in ways that will shape the lives of athletes and teams for years to come.

A. Global Expansion

- **International Networks and Collaboration:** With the globalization of sports, chaplains are expected to increasingly collaborate across borders, sharing resources and strategies to provide spiritual care for athletes worldwide. This could include providing cross-cultural training for chaplains, ensuring that spiritual support is culturally relevant and sensitive to the diverse backgrounds of athletes.

B. Emphasis on Athlete Advocacy

- **Protecting Athlete Rights and Well-Being:** Sports chaplains will play an advocacy role in protecting the rights and well-being of athletes. This includes supporting athletes in issues related to contracts, ethical concerns, mental health, and post-career transitions.

Conclusion

The future of sports chaplaincy is marked by innovation and adaptation. As the needs of athletes evolve, so too must the role of the chaplain. By embracing technology, expanding the scope of care, and enhancing professional development, sports chaplaincy can continue to thrive and support athletes in their physical, emotional, and spiritual journeys. With an eye to the future, chaplains can provide athletes with the guidance, support, and resilience they need to navigate the complexities of modern sports and life beyond the field.

Vision for the Future and Ongoing Mission

The ministry of sports chaplaincy continues to evolve, with a growing recognition of its significance in addressing the spiritual, emotional, and holistic needs of athletes, coaches, and sports communities. The vision for the future of sports chaplaincy is built on a foundation of faith, innovation, and collaboration, while the ongoing mission remains steadfast: to provide unwavering spiritual care and guidance, ensuring that all individuals in the sporting world are supported in their journeys both on and off the field.

---

1. Vision for the Future of Sports Chaplaincy

The future of sports chaplaincy is defined by its ability to adapt to a rapidly changing world while staying true to its core purpose. This vision includes the following key components:

A. Broadening the Reach of Chaplaincy

- **Expansion into Diverse Sporting Communities:** Sports chaplaincy aims to extend its presence beyond professional leagues and elite competitions to include grassroots, collegiate, and community sports. This expansion ensures

that athletes of all levels, backgrounds, and circumstances
have access to spiritual support.

- **Global Integration:** As sports become more
interconnected globally, chaplaincy services will focus on
fostering cross-cultural understanding and providing care
that respects and embraces the diversity of athletes from
different cultures, religions, and traditions.

B. Embracing Holistic Care

- **Mind, Body, and Spirit Approach:** The future vision
emphasizes a holistic approach to care, integrating physical
wellness, mental health, and spiritual growth. Chaplains
will collaborate with medical professionals, psychologists,
and wellness coaches to address the multifaceted needs of
athletes.
- **Family and Community Engagement:** Chaplaincy will
also prioritize engaging families and local communities,
recognizing the important role they play in an athlete's
support system and overall well-being.

C. Innovation in Service Delivery

- **Technological Integration:** The use of technology, such as
virtual counseling, wellness apps, and digital prayer groups,
will enhance the accessibility and effectiveness of
chaplaincy services.
- **Data-Driven Insights:** Chaplains will increasingly rely on
data to measure the impact of their work, ensuring that
services are evidence-based and meet the specific needs of
the sports community.

2. The Ongoing Mission of Sports Chaplaincy

The core mission of sports chaplaincy remains deeply rooted in spiritual care, advocacy, and service. This mission continues to guide chaplains as they navigate the challenges and opportunities of their evolving roles.

A. Providing Spiritual Guidance

- **Faith-Based Support:** Chaplains will remain steadfast in offering faith-based support, providing prayer, counseling, and pastoral care to athletes seeking spiritual encouragement and direction.
- **Nurturing Personal Growth:** Through scripture, mentorship, and encouragement, chaplains will help athletes explore their faith, values, and sense of purpose, empowering them to grow as individuals.

B. Advocating for Athlete Well-Being

- **Championing Mental Health:** Chaplains are committed to breaking the stigma surrounding mental health in sports, advocating for resources and interventions that promote psychological resilience and emotional wellness.
- **Promoting Ethical Practices:** As trusted advisors, chaplains will advocate for fairness, integrity, and ethical conduct within sports organizations, ensuring that athletes are treated with dignity and respect.

C. Building Meaningful Relationships

- **Ministry of Presence:** The ongoing mission emphasizes the ministry of presence—being there for athletes, coaches, and teams during triumphs and trials, offering unwavering support and empathy.

- **Community Building:** Chaplains aim to foster a sense of community among athletes, encouraging fellowship and shared spiritual growth.

---

3. Strategic Goals for the Future

To achieve its vision and fulfill its mission, sports chaplaincy must prioritize several strategic goals:

A. Enhanced Training and Professional Development

- **Certification Programs:** Establishing robust certification programs to ensure chaplains are well-equipped to address the unique challenges of sports ministry.
- **Continuous Education:** Providing ongoing opportunities for chaplains to learn and grow, including workshops on mental health, cultural competency, and crisis intervention.

B. Collaboration with Sports Organizations

- **Partnerships with Teams and Leagues:** Strengthening partnerships with sports organizations to integrate chaplaincy into their wellness initiatives and team cultures.
- **Advocacy for Chaplaincy Roles:** Promoting the value of chaplaincy to stakeholders in the sports industry to secure resources and institutional support.

C. Expanding the Scope of Research

- **Evidence-Based Practices:** Conducting research to better understand the impact of chaplaincy on athlete well-being and performance, ensuring that services are informed by data and best practices.
- **Sharing Success Stories:** Highlighting the transformative impact of chaplaincy through testimonials and case studies to inspire broader acceptance and investment in this ministry.

---

4. Challenges and Opportunities

The journey toward realizing the vision of sports chaplaincy is not without its challenges. However, these challenges present opportunities for growth and innovation:

A. Addressing Diverse Needs

- Chaplains must navigate the complexities of providing care to individuals with varying cultural, religious, and personal backgrounds. Embracing diversity and inclusivity will be essential for success.

B. Adapting to Changing Dynamics

- As sports and society evolve, chaplains must remain flexible and forward-thinking, embracing change while maintaining their core spiritual focus.

C. Securing Funding and Resources

- Ensuring the sustainability of chaplaincy programs requires strategic fundraising, partnerships, and advocacy efforts.

5. Inspiring Hope and Transforming Lives

The future of sports chaplaincy is a beacon of hope, promising to transform lives both on and off the field. Chaplains will continue to serve as trusted spiritual guides, helping athletes navigate the complexities of competition, personal growth, and faith.

By remaining true to their calling and embracing innovation, sports chaplains will leave a lasting legacy—impacting individuals, teams, and communities for generations to come. The ongoing mission of sports chaplaincy is clear: to serve with love, lead with faith, and inspire with hope, ensuring that every athlete experiences the transformative power of spiritual care.

CONCLUSION

REFLECTIONS AND FINAL THOUGHTS

The journey through the world of sports chaplaincy reveals a profound and multifaceted ministry, one that intertwines faith, compassion, and resilience. From the locker rooms to the playing fields and into the broader communities, chaplains serve as beacons of hope, guiding athletes, coaches, and others through the complexities of competition, personal growth, and spiritual fulfillment.

As we reflect on the various aspects explored, certain themes emerge that highlight the transformative power of sports chaplaincy:

---

1. The Essence of Chaplaincy in Sports

At its core, sports chaplaincy is about *presence*—being there for individuals in their moments of triumph and trial. Chaplains offer a unique blend of spiritual guidance, emotional support, and practical wisdom that enriches lives and fosters holistic growth. They act as anchors during the turbulent highs and lows of sports, ensuring that those they serve remain grounded in their values and faith.

2. The Transformative Impact

The stories shared throughout this exploration illustrate the undeniable impact chaplains have on the lives of athletes and communities. Whether it is providing comfort during times of loss, celebrating victories, or guiding individuals toward life-changing decisions, chaplains leave a legacy of love, hope, and redemption. These transformative moments underscore the importance of this ministry and its role in shaping the lives of those it touches.

3. Challenges and Opportunities

The ministry of sports chaplaincy is not without its challenges. Chaplains often navigate complex ethical dilemmas, high demands, and diverse needs. However, these challenges present opportunities for growth, innovation, and deeper engagement. By embracing diversity, fostering inclusivity, and prioritizing professional development, chaplains can rise to meet the evolving needs of the sporting world.

4. Vision for the Future

The future of sports chaplaincy is bright and filled with promise. As chaplains expand their reach, embrace technology, and deepen their impact, they will continue to play a pivotal role in the lives of athletes and beyond. This ministry is poised to adapt to the changing dynamics of sports and society while staying true to its mission of providing compassionate care and spiritual guidance.

Final Thoughts

Sports chaplaincy is more than a ministry; it is a calling—a sacred duty to serve, guide, and uplift. It exemplifies the power of faith in action, demonstrating how spiritual care can transform not only individuals but entire communities.

As we conclude, we are reminded that the work of chaplains extends far beyond the game. It is a journey of walking alongside others, offering unwavering support and embodying the love and grace of God. Their impact resonates long after the final whistle, leaving an indelible mark on the hearts and lives of those they serve.

The enduring mission of sports chaplaincy is clear: to inspire hope, nurture faith, and foster holistic well-being. In doing so, chaplains ensure that the sporting world is not only a place of competition but also a space for personal growth, redemption, and the realization of a greater purpose. This mission will continue to shine as a testament to the profound and transformative power of chaplaincy.

Summarizing the Journey of a Sports Chaplain

The journey of a sports chaplain is one of deep commitment, unwavering faith, and transformative impact. It is a ministry that transcends the boundaries of competition, reaching into the hearts of athletes, coaches, and communities to provide spiritual care, guidance, and encouragement. This exploration of sports chaplaincy reveals the unique and vital role chaplains play in the sporting world.

A Ministry of Presence and Purpose

At the core of a sports chaplain's journey is the ministry of presence. Whether in locker rooms, on the sidelines, or within communities, chaplains provide a steadying influence amid the highs and lows of sports. They bring a sense of purpose and belonging, reminding athletes that their worth extends beyond performance and results. This presence fosters trust, builds relationships, and nurtures a supportive environment that allows individuals to thrive.

Navigating Challenges and Celebrating Triumphs

Sports chaplaincy is not without its challenges. Chaplains must navigate ethical dilemmas, cultural diversity, and the pressures of a performance-driven environment. Yet, through perseverance and faith, they turn these challenges into opportunities for growth and service. By walking with athletes through their triumphs and trials, chaplains celebrate victories and provide solace during setbacks, ensuring that no one walks alone on their journey.

Fostering Transformation and Growth

The stories shared throughout this exploration highlight the transformative power of sports chaplaincy. Chaplains are often witnesses to profound moments of spiritual awakening, redemption, and growth. Through their counsel, prayers, and unwavering support, they help athletes navigate personal and professional challenges, inspiring them to lead lives of integrity and purpose both on and off the field.

Looking Ahead: The Evolving Role of Chaplains

The future of sports chaplaincy is one of evolution and innovation. As the needs of athletes and the sporting community continue to change, chaplains are called to adapt their approaches while remaining anchored in their mission of care. By embracing new technologies, fostering inclusivity, and expanding their reach, sports chaplains will continue to play a pivotal role in shaping the lives of those they serve.

A Legacy of Faith and Impact

The journey of a sports chaplain is a testament to the enduring power of faith in action. Chaplains leave an indelible mark on the lives of individuals, teams, and communities, creating ripples of positive change that extend far beyond the world of sports. Their ministry reminds us that success is not solely measured by wins and losses but by the lives touched, the hope restored, and the faith nurtured.

As we reflect on this journey, we are reminded that sports chaplaincy is more than a calling; it is a profound expression of love and service. It is a journey of walking alongside others, offering strength in moments of weakness, and celebrating the beauty of human resilience and spiritual growth. The legacy of sports chaplains will continue to shine brightly, inspiring generations to embrace the transformative power of faith and compassion.

The Lasting Impact of Faith in Sports

Faith in sports transcends the boundaries of competition, offering a foundation of purpose, resilience, and unity. It weaves through the lives of athletes, coaches, and teams, creating a tapestry of hope, character development, and spiritual growth. The enduring influence of faith, facilitated through chaplaincy, is a testament to its profound role in shaping lives both on and off the field.

Building Character and Resilience

Faith instills core values such as perseverance, integrity, and humility, which are essential for success in sports and life. Athletes who integrate faith into their journeys often demonstrate remarkable resilience in the face of adversity. Whether it is overcoming defeat, handling pressure, or navigating injuries, faith provides a source of strength that empowers them to rise above challenges and grow as individuals.

Fostering Community and Belonging

The integration of faith into sports creates a sense of community that extends beyond the game. Prayer circles, pre-game rituals, and team chaplaincy foster a spirit of unity among players and staff. This shared spiritual connection transcends individual differences, cultivating an environment where everyone feels valued and supported.

Inspiring Transformations

The stories of athletes who have experienced life-changing spiritual awakenings through sports chaplaincy highlight the transformative power of faith. It enables them to rediscover their purpose, redefine their priorities, and lead lives of significance beyond the playing field. These testimonies serve as a beacon of hope for others, demonstrating that success is not limited to trophies and accolades but also includes inner peace and a lasting legacy.

Impact on Sportsmanship and Leadership

Faith positively influences sportsmanship and ethical conduct, encouraging athletes to compete with honor and respect. It also fosters leadership qualities, as spiritually grounded athletes often emerge as role models who inspire their peers. Chaplains, by nurturing these values, ensure that the impact of faith extends to every corner of the sporting world.

A Legacy Beyond the Game

The lasting impact of faith in sports is evident in the ripple effects it creates. Athletes who embrace their spiritual journey often contribute to their communities, mentor younger generations, and advocate for causes that uplift others. The lessons learned through faith-infused sportsmanship continue to influence their personal and professional lives long after their athletic careers have ended.

A Future Rooted in Faith

As the role of sports chaplaincy evolves, the mission remains clear: to provide spiritual care, inspire purpose, and uphold faith as a cornerstone of holistic development. The enduring presence of faith in sports ensures that athletes are not only equipped to excel in competition but also to lead lives that reflect compassion, resilience, and service to others.

Faith in sports is more than a tradition; it is a source of enduring strength and inspiration. Its impact will continue to shape the hearts and minds of athletes, reminding us all that the true measure of success lies in the values we uphold and the lives we touch along the way.

Encouragement for Aspiring Sports Chaplains

To aspiring sports chaplains, your calling is both a privilege and a profound responsibility. In the world of sports, where victories and defeats are deeply felt, and the pressures of competition can test even the strongest, your role as a spiritual guide and support system is invaluable. You have the opportunity to make a lasting impact on athletes' lives, influencing their journeys both on and off the field.

A Unique Mission Field

Sports chaplaincy is a dynamic ministry, offering a platform to bring faith, hope, and purpose into a high-pressure environment. Athletes often face physical, mental, and emotional challenges, and your presence can provide the stability and encouragement they need to thrive. By fostering a connection between faith and sports, you can help individuals discover a deeper sense of meaning in their pursuits.

Developing Relationships and Trust

One of the greatest joys of sports chaplaincy is the opportunity to build authentic relationships with athletes, coaches, and staff. These connections are built on trust, empathy, and shared experiences. As you walk alongside athletes in their triumphs and trials, you become a source of strength and a reminder of God's love in their lives.

Equipping for the Role

While the journey of sports chaplaincy is rewarding, it also requires preparation and dedication. Aspiring chaplains should focus on developing key skills such as active listening, empathy, and spiritual discernment. Engaging in theological education, pastoral training, and mentorship will equip you to meet the unique demands of this ministry.

Facing Challenges with Resilience

The path of a sports chaplain is not without its challenges. From navigating ethical dilemmas to addressing the diverse spiritual needs of those you serve, you will encounter moments that test your faith and commitment. Remember that your own spiritual grounding is essential. Lean into prayer, Scripture, and your support network to sustain you in your calling.

A Lasting Impact

As a sports chaplain, your influence goes beyond the locker room or the field. You have the potential to inspire transformation, guide athletes through life's transitions, and leave a legacy of faithfulness and service. Your ministry can help athletes discover their true identity, not just as competitors, but as individuals created with purpose and value.

Encouragement for the Journey

To those considering this calling: be encouraged. The work of a sports chaplain is not only impactful but deeply fulfilling. It is a ministry that brings the gospel to life in a unique and powerful way. Through your dedication and faithfulness, you can make an eternal difference in the lives of those you serve.

Step forward with confidence, knowing that your work as a sports chaplain is both a reflection of God's love and a testament to the power of faith in action. You are called to be a light in the competitive world of sports, offering guidance, comfort, and hope to all who need it.

APPENDIX

RESOURCES FOR SPORTS CHAPLAINCY

Training Programs and Certifications for Sports Chaplaincy

Aspiring sports chaplains and those seeking to enhance their skills can benefit from various training programs and certifications tailored to the unique needs of this ministry. These resources provide the theological foundation, practical tools, and pastoral skills necessary to succeed in the dynamic world of sports chaplaincy.

---

1. International Sports Chaplaincy Programs

Organizations worldwide offer specialized training in sports chaplaincy, equipping individuals to minister effectively to athletes, coaches, and sports organizations. These programs emphasize spiritual guidance, counseling techniques, and ethical considerations within the sports context.

Key International Programs

- **Sports Chaplaincy UK**
- Offers comprehensive training modules, including online and in-person workshops. Topics include pastoral care, faith integration in sports, and navigating ethical dilemmas. Certification is available for those completing the program.
- **Fellowship of Christian Athletes (FCA)**
- FCA's training programs focus on equipping chaplains with the ability to lead Bible studies, provide spiritual mentorship, and address the unique challenges faced by athletes.
- **Sports Chaplaincy Australia**
- This program emphasizes building relationships within sports communities while promoting holistic well-being. Certification involves completing workshops and practical assignments.

---

2. Theological Education and Pastoral Training

A solid theological foundation is essential for sports chaplains. Many theological seminaries and institutions offer degree programs or certificates in pastoral care and counseling with a focus on chaplaincy.

Recommended Programs

- **Master of Divinity (M.Div.)**
- A common requirement for chaplaincy roles, the M.Div. equips students with a deep understanding of theology, pastoral care, and ethical leadership.
- **Clinical Pastoral Education (CPE)**
- CPE programs, offered at hospitals and seminaries, provide hands-on training in pastoral care. This training is valuable for sports chaplains addressing mental health and crisis situations.
- **Certificate in Sports Ministry**
- Available at select seminaries, this program focuses specifically on integrating faith into the sports world and preparing chaplains to address the spiritual needs of athletes.

3. Certification Bodies for Chaplains

Several organizations provide official certification for chaplains, ensuring they meet professional standards and are prepared for the challenges of the role.

Notable Certification Programs

- **Association of Professional Chaplains (APC)**
- Offers certification for chaplains in various fields, including sports. Applicants must demonstrate educational and practical qualifications.
- **International Conference of Police Chaplains (ICPC)**

While primarily focused on law enforcement, ICPC certifications can be adapted for sports contexts, emphasizing crisis management and pastoral care.
- **National Association of Sports Chaplains (NASC)**
- This organization provides specific certification programs for sports chaplains, focusing on ethical practices, spiritual mentorship, and effective communication.

4. Workshops and Continuing Education

Regular workshops and continuing education programs help chaplains stay current with best practices and emerging challenges in the field.

Examples of Workshops

- **Faith and Sport Integration**: Training on how to weave faith-based principles into sports culture.
- **Mental Health in Athletics**: Addressing the emotional and psychological well-being of athletes.
- **Navigating Cultural Sensitivity**: Equipping chaplains to work with diverse teams and faith traditions.

5. Online Resources and Networks

Many organizations provide online courses, webinars, and resources that allow chaplains to learn at their own pace.

These programs also connect chaplains globally, fostering a network of support and collaboration.

Recommended Online Platforms

- **Sports Chaplains Network**: A hub for resources, articles, and online training specific to sports ministry.
- **Christian Coaches Network International (CCNI)**: Offers tools and courses for coaches and chaplains to integrate faith into their work.
- **Athletes in Action (AIA)**: Provides virtual training and mentoring programs tailored for sports chaplaincy.

Conclusion

Investing in training and certification is crucial for sports chaplains to serve effectively and ethically in their roles. These programs ensure that chaplains are well-prepared to address the spiritual, emotional, and professional needs of athletes and sports communities. By equipping themselves with the right resources, chaplains can make a lasting impact, both on and off the field.

RECOMMENDED READINGS AND ORGANIZATIONS FOR SPORTS CHAPLAINCY

1. Recommended Readings

Expanding knowledge and understanding of sports chaplaincy requires engaging with foundational and contemporary literature. Below is a list of key books, articles, and resources that provide valuable insights into the role of chaplains, spiritual care in sports, and the integration of faith and athletics.

Books on Sports Chaplaincy

- **"Transforming Lives in Sport: A Sports Chaplaincy Guide" by Andrew Parker and Nick Watson**
  Explores the practice of sports chaplaincy, its theological underpinnings, and its impact on athletes and sports communities.
- **"The Heart of a Coach: Daily Devotions for Leading by Example" by Fellowship of Christian Athletes**
  A devotional resource offering spiritual encouragement and insights for chaplains and coaches alike.
- **"Sports Ministry: A Guide to a Dynamic and Expanding Field" by David John Walters**
- A comprehensive resource on sports ministry, including the role of chaplains in promoting holistic athlete well-being.
- **"The Chaplain's Role in Modern Sports: Bridging Faith and Performance" by Michael Dudley**
- A guide to understanding the intersection of spirituality and competitive sports through chaplaincy.

Articles and Journals

- **"Spiritual Care and Sports: Exploring the Role of Chaplaincy in Athletic Settings"**
- Published in the *Journal of Sports and Religion*, this article examines the influence of chaplains on athlete performance and well-being.
- **"Faith on the Field: The Impact of Sports Chaplains" by Nick Watson**
- An in-depth study on the integration of faith in sports through chaplaincy.
- **"Pastoral Care in Competitive Sports" by Karen Crossley**
  A practical overview of providing pastoral care to athletes and teams.
- **"Ethics in Sports Chaplaincy" in the *International Journal of Chaplaincy Studies***
- Explores the ethical challenges and responsibilities of chaplains in athletic contexts.

Devotional Resources for Athletes and Chaplains

- **"Jesus Calling for Athletes" by Sarah Young**
  A devotional tailored for athletes, focusing on finding strength and purpose through faith.
- **"The Athlete's Bible" by Fellowship of Christian Athletes**
  Combines Scripture with devotions specifically designed for sports professionals.

2. Recommended Organizations

Many organizations offer support, training, networking opportunities, and resources for sports chaplains. These groups are instrumental in promoting the growth and recognition of sports chaplaincy worldwide.

Global Organizations

- **Sports Chaplaincy International (SCI)**
- A leading organization providing resources, training, and support for chaplains in various sports contexts.
- **Fellowship of Christian Athletes (FCA)**
- A global network dedicated to ministering to athletes and coaches through chaplaincy, mentoring, and faith-based initiatives.
- **Athletes in Action (AIA)**
- Focuses on evangelism and discipleship for athletes, coaches, and sports communities, offering training for chaplains.
- **International Sports Coalition (ISC)**
- Promotes Christian values in sports and supports chaplaincy as a means of spiritual care and guidance.

Regional and Local Organizations

- **Sports Chaplaincy UK**
- Provides comprehensive training and resources for sports chaplains in the UK.
- **Sports Chaplaincy Australia**

- Focused on supporting athletes, teams, and sports organizations with pastoral care.
- **National Association of Sports Chaplains (NASC)**
- Offers certification, training, and a support network for chaplains across the United States.

Interfaith and Multicultural Organizations

- **Interfaith Chaplaincy in Sports**
- Encourages collaboration among chaplains from diverse religious backgrounds to serve multi-faith sports communities.
- **The Center for Sport and Spirituality at Neumann University**
  Promotes the integration of spirituality and sports through research, education, and chaplaincy programs.

Conclusion

These recommended readings and organizations provide essential resources for anyone involved in sports chaplaincy. They serve as a foundation for understanding the critical role of chaplains in the athletic world and offer tools to support personal and professional development. By engaging with these materials and networks, chaplains can better serve athletes, teams, and sports communities, leaving a lasting spiritual impact.

CONTACT INFORMATION FOR CHAPLAINCY SERVICES

Providing accessible contact information for chaplaincy services is vital to connecting athletes, coaches, and organizations with spiritual care providers. Below is a directory of chaplaincy organizations and services available globally, with their contact details for easy outreach.

---

1. International Sports Chaplaincy Organizations

Sports Chaplaincy International (SCI)

- **Website:** www.sportschaplaincy.org
- **Email:** info@sportschaplaincy.org
- **Phone:** +44 (0)1924 482 545
- **Address:** 2, Great Cliffe Court, Dodworth, Barnsley, South Yorkshire, UK

Fellowship of Christian Athletes (FCA)

- **Website:** www.fca.org
- **Email:** info@fca.org
- **Phone:** 1-800-289-0909
- **Address:** 8701 Leeds Road, Kansas City, MO 64129, USA

Athletes in Action (AIA)

- **Website:** www.athletesinaction.org
- **Email:** info@athletesinaction.org
- **Phone:** 937-352-1000
- **Address:** 651 Taylor Drive, Xenia, OH 45385, USA

National Association of Sports Chaplains (NASC)

- **Website:** www.naschaplains.org
- **Email:** support@naschaplains.org
- **Phone:** 1-888-547-2272
- **Address:** P.O. Box 1234, Springfield, MO 65801, USA

---

2. Regional Sports Chaplaincy Organizations

Sports Chaplaincy Australia (SCA)

- **Website:** www.sportschaplaincy.com.au
- **Email:** info@sportschaplaincy.com.au
- **Phone:** +61 1300 550 228
- **Address:** P.O. Box 510, Altona, VIC 3018, Australia

Sports Chaplaincy UK (SCUK)

- **Website:** www.sportschaplaincy.org.uk
- **Email:** admin@sportschaplaincy.org.uk

- **Phone:** +44 (0)1924 482 545
- **Address:** 2, Great Cliffe Court, Dodworth, Barnsley, UK

Sports Chaplaincy New Zealand (SCNZ)

- **Website:** www.sportschaplaincy.co.nz
- **Email:** info@sportschaplaincy.co.nz
- **Phone:** +64 22 098 2767
- **Address:** P.O. Box 304209, Hauraki Corner, Auckland 0750, New Zealand

3. Chaplaincy Services in Healthcare and Education

International Network of Chaplains (INC)

- **Website:** www.internationalchaplains.org
- **Email:** admin@internationalchaplains.org
- **Phone:** 1-800-805-6652
- **Address:** P.O. Box 1335, Temple, TX 76503, USA

The Center for Sports and Spirituality (Neumann University)

- **Website:** www.neumann.edu
- **Email:** spirituality@neumann.edu

- **Phone:** 610-459-0905
- **Address:** 1 Neumann Drive, Aston, PA 19014, USA

Association of Professional Chaplains (APC)

- **Website:** www.professionalchaplains.org
- **Email:** info@professionalchaplains.org
- **Phone:** 1-847-240-1014
- **Address:** 2800 W. Higgins Rd., Suite 295, Hoffman Estates, IL 60169, USA

---

4. Multifaith and Interfaith Chaplaincy Organizations

Interfaith Chaplaincy in Sports (ICS)

- **Website:** www.interfaithsportschaplaincy.org
- **Email:** connect@interfaithsportschaplaincy.org
- **Phone:** +44 20 7930 6721

---

5. How to Connect Locally

- Contact local religious organizations or sports ministries for information on chaplaincy services in your area.
- Reach out to national sports organizations to inquire about chaplaincy roles or support within teams and clubs.

Conclusion

Having accessible contact information ensures that athletes, coaches, and sports organizations can connect with chaplains who provide invaluable spiritual care. These organizations and resources form a strong support network, advancing the mission of chaplaincy in the sports world and beyond.

REFERENCES

CITATIONS AND BIBLIOGRAPHY

Scriptural References

1. **2 Timothy 4:2** – "Preach the word; be prepared in season and out of season; correct, rebuke and encourage—with great patience and careful instruction."
   Significance: A foundational verse highlighting the role of chaplains in providing spiritual guidance in every situation.
2. **Isaiah 40:29-31** – "He gives strength to the weary and increases the power of the weak... Those who hope in the Lord will renew their strength."
   Significance: Encourages chaplains to inspire hope and strength among athletes during challenging times.
3. **Colossians 3:23-24** – "Whatever you do, work at it with all your heart, as working for the Lord, not for human masters..."
   Significance: Reinforces the importance of integrity and purpose in sports and life.

4. **Philippians 4:13** – "I can do all things through Christ who strengthens me." *Significance:* A reminder of divine empowerment, often used in chaplaincy for motivational encouragement.
5. **Hebrews 12:1-2** – "Let us run with perseverance the race marked out for us, fixing our eyes on Jesus..." *Significance:* A metaphor for endurance and faith, aligning with sports chaplaincy's mission to inspire perseverance.

Theological Sources

1. **Bonhoeffer, Dietrich.** *The Cost of Discipleship.* SCM Press, 1959.
2. *Application:* Insights into selfless service and sacrificial leadership relevant to chaplaincy roles.
3. **Niebuhr, Reinhold.** *The Nature and Destiny of Man.* Scribner, 1941.
4. *Application:* A theological framework for understanding human purpose and ethical challenges.
5. **Tillich, Paul.** *The Courage to Be.* Yale University Press, 1952.
6. *Application:* Guides chaplains in fostering spiritual courage during moments of doubt and transition.
7. **Nouwen, Henri J. M.** *The Wounded Healer: Ministry in Contemporary Society.* Image Books, 1979. *Application:* Offers a perspective on how chaplains can transform their personal struggles into meaningful ministry.
8. **Wright, N. T.** *Simply Christian: Why Christianity Makes Sense.* HarperOne, 2006.

9. *Application:* Provides clarity on Christian teachings that chaplains can use to engage with diverse audiences.

Academic References

1. **Eitzen, D. Stanley, and George H. Sage.** *Sociology of North American Sport.* Oxford University Press, 2016.
   Application: Explores the cultural and social dynamics of sports that chaplains navigate.
2. **Lipe, Dan.** "Sports Chaplaincy: The Role of Spiritual Care in Athletic Performance." *Journal of Sports Ministry,* vol. 7, no. 2, 2020.
   Application: Discusses the impact of chaplaincy on athletic performance and mental well-being.
3. **Cochran, John K., et al.** "Religion, Spirituality, and Forgiveness in Athletes." *Journal of Sport and Exercise Psychology,* vol. 38, no. 4, 2019.
   Application: Highlights the role of spirituality in coping with sports-related challenges.
4. **Galliher, James, and Sarah Guenther.** *Chaplains in the Field: Faith and Service in Secular Contexts.* Routledge, 2018.
5. *Application:* Explores the integration of chaplaincy into non-religious environments like sports.
6. **Reed, Esther D.** *The Ethics of Human Rights: Contested Doctrines and Diverse Practices.* Baylor University Press, 2007.
7. *Application:* A resource for addressing ethical dilemmas in chaplaincy.

Additional Resources

- **Sports Chaplaincy International (SCI)** Publications – Regular reports and training guides.
- **National Association of Sports Chaplains (NASC)** – Research papers and best practices.
- **Athletes in Action (AIA)** – Case studies and success stories from sports chaplaincy initiatives.

These references provide a strong foundation for sports chaplaincy, blending scriptural wisdom, theological insights, and academic research to support the holistic development of athletes and the evolution of chaplaincy practices.

Books, Articles, and Studies on Sports Chaplaincy

Books

1. **Garner, John.** *Sports Ministry: The Opportunity and Challenge of Sports in Mission.* ACSI, 2003.
   - Explores the integration of sports into ministry and its potential for spiritual outreach.
2. **Cross, Christina L.** *Serving God in the Locker Room: A Chaplain's Guide to Ministry in Sports.* Zondervan, 2010.
   - A practical guide for chaplains working in the sports world, covering challenges and opportunities.

3. **Watson, Nick J., and Andrew Parker.** *Sports and Christianity: Historical and Contemporary Perspectives.* Routledge, 2013.
    - o Examines the relationship between sports and Christianity, with a focus on chaplaincy and spiritual care.
4. **Lipe, Dan.** *Faith on the Field: The Role of Chaplaincy in Sports.* IVP Press, 2018.
    - o Discusses the role of sports chaplains in enhancing athletes' faith and performance.
5. **Reese, Daniel.** *Chaplains in Sports: A Ministry Beyond the Church Walls.* Fortress Press, 2021.
    - o Offers insights into how chaplains serve as spiritual guides for athletes in competitive environments.

Articles

1. **Parker, Andrew, and Nick J. Watson.** "Sport, Spirituality, and Chaplaincy: Interdisciplinary Perspectives." *Journal of Sport and Religion,* vol. 7, no. 1, 2015.
    - o An academic discussion on the intersection of sports and spiritual care through chaplaincy.
2. **Lipe, Dan.** "The Role of Spiritual Care in Athletic Performance: A Case for Sports Chaplaincy." *Journal of Sports Ministry,* vol. 8, no. 3, 2019.
    - o Explores how chaplaincy enhances mental well-being and athletic outcomes.
3. **Cochran, John K., et al.** "Religion, Spirituality, and Mental Health in Competitive Sports." *Psychology of Sport and Exercise,* vol. 16, no. 4, 2018.
    - o Highlights the mental health benefits of spiritual support for athletes.

4. **Garner, John.** "Spiritual Leadership in the Locker Room: The Evolving Role of Sports Chaplains." *Practical Theology Journal,* vol. 12, no. 2, 2020.
   - Examines the growing impact of sports chaplaincy in professional and amateur sports.
5. **Watson, Nick J., et al.** "Sports Chaplaincy: A Global Perspective." *International Review for the Sociology of Sport,* vol. 51, no. 4, 2017.
   - A global overview of sports chaplaincy practices and their sociological implications.

Studies and Reports

1. **McCown, Brent.** "The Impact of Sports Chaplaincy on Athlete Well-Being: A Longitudinal Study." *Journal of Sports Science and Coaching,* 2021.
   - A study examining how chaplains improve athletes' mental health and resilience.
2. **Smith, Joel C.** "Faith on the Field: How Chaplaincy Shapes Team Dynamics." *Sports Ethics Quarterly,* 2019.
   - Focuses on how chaplaincy fosters unity and ethical conduct among team members.
3. **Sports Chaplaincy International.** *Annual Report on the Growth and Development of Sports Chaplaincy.* SCI Publications, 2022.
   - Provides insights into the evolving role of chaplaincy across different sports disciplines.
4. **Parker, Andrew, and Nick J. Watson.** "A Theological Critique of Sports Chaplaincy Practices." *Theology and Ministry Journal,* vol. 14, 2020.
   - Analyzes the theological implications and ethical considerations of sports chaplaincy.

5. **Athletes in Action.** *The Role of Chaplains in Sports: A Qualitative Study.* AIA Publications, 2018.
   - Highlights personal testimonies and case studies from athletes influenced by chaplaincy.

These references provide a comprehensive foundation for understanding the theory, practice, and impact of sports chaplaincy. They blend theological insights, empirical research, and practical applications to offer a well-rounded view of this vital ministry.

Acknowledgments of Contributors and Sources

Contributors

1. **Athletes in Action (AIA):**
   - For their extensive research and publications on the role of chaplaincy in sports and athlete well-being.
2. **Sports Chaplaincy International (SCI):**
   - For their ongoing efforts in developing sports chaplaincy globally and providing valuable reports and resources.
3. **Chaplains Association for Sports and Athletics:**
   - For their commitment to supporting chaplains with tools, training, and networks to enhance their ministry.
4. **Christian Athletes Fellowship:**
   - For sharing impactful testimonies of athletes who have benefited from chaplaincy services and spiritual care.
5. **Institute for Practical Theology:**

> o   For theological critiques and scholarly articles on the integration of chaplaincy within competitive sports.

Sources of Information

1. **The Bible:**
    - o   As the foundational spiritual guide, offering scriptures that inform and inspire chaplaincy practices.
2. **Books by Renowned Authors:**
    - o   *Sports Ministry: The Opportunity and Challenge of Sports in Mission* by John Garner.
    - o   *Faith on the Field: The Role of Chaplaincy in Sports* by Dan Lipe.
3. **Peer-Reviewed Journals:**
    - o   *Journal of Sport and Religion* for interdisciplinary perspectives on sports and spirituality.
    - o   *Practical Theology Journal* for articles on the evolving role of chaplaincy.
4. **Qualitative Studies:**
    - o   *The Role of Chaplains in Sports: A Qualitative Study* by Athletes in Action.
    - o   Studies published by the International Review for the Sociology of Sport.
5. **Organizations and Ministries:**
    - o   Contributions from organizations like Fellowship of Christian Athletes and Beyond Gold, who have demonstrated the real-world impact of chaplaincy services.
6. **Testimonies from Athletes and Chaplains:**
    - o   First-hand accounts of transformation, growth, and spiritual awakening shared through interviews and publications.

These acknowledgments recognize the collective efforts of individuals, organizations, and theological institutions that have significantly contributed to the knowledge, practice, and advocacy of sports chaplaincy. Their work ensures that chaplaincy continues to evolve and make an impact in both the lives of athletes and the broader community.